Thomas J. Wright

History of the Eighth regiment Kentucky vol. inf.,

During its three years campaigns, embracing organization, marches, skirmishes, and battles of the command, with much of the history of the old reliable Third brigade, commanded by Hon. Stanley Matthe

Thomas J. Wright

History of the Eighth regiment Kentucky vol. inf.,
During its three years campaigns, embracing organization, marches, skirmishes, and battles of the command, with much of the history of the old reliable Third brigade, commanded by Hon. Stanley Matthe

ISBN/EAN: 9783337810542

Printed in Europe, USA, Canada, Australia, Japan

Cover: Foto ©ninafisch / pixelio.de

More available books at **www.hansebooks.com**

HISTORY

OF THE

EIGHTH REGIMENT

KENTUCKY VOL. INF.,

DURING ITS

THREE YEARS CAMPAIGNS

EMBRACING

Organization, Marches, Skirmishes,

AND

Battles of the Command,

WITH

MUCH OF THE HISTORY OF THE OLD RELIABLE THIRD
BRIGADE, COMMANDED BY HON. STANLEY MAT-
THEWS, AND CONTAINING MANY

INTERESTING AND AMUSING INCIDENTS OF
ARMY LIFE.

By CAPT. T. J. WRIGHT.

ST. JOSEPH, MO.:
ST. JOSEPH STEAM PRINTING COMPANY,
1880.

Entered according to Act of Congress in the year 1880 by
CAPT. T. J. WRIGHT.

TO THE
MEMORY OF MY FORMER COMRADES,
WHO DEFENDED OUR GLORIOUS UNION,
IN THE
WAR AGAINST REBELLION,
WHETHER THEY FELL UPON THE BATTLEFIELD,
OR WASTED AWAY
FROM WOUNDS AND DISEASE IN HOSPITALS AND PRISONS
WHETHER THEY LIE
BURIED IN LONELY SOUTHERN GRAVES,
OR
RETURNED HOME WITH SHATTERED CONSTITUTIONS,
TO SUFFER AND
SINK INTO UNTIMELY GRAVES,
THIS VOLUME
IS MOST AFFECTIONATELY DEDICATED
BY
THE AUTHOR.

PREFACE.

In placing this History before the public, the author takes pleasure in assuring his readers that this work is not fiction, but a chronological order of facts, wherein runs along the wild tide of war and great events; of fields of blood; the comparative succeeding calm; of the soldier's daily toils, camp duties and privations; their many hardships, marches, skirmishes and battles; detailing modes of cooking, with many amusing episodes of foraging expeditions, being truly the true inwardness of the private soldier's life. Written from the author's daily journal, kept by him throughout this Veteran Regiment's long and eventful service, embracing much of the history of the renowned Third Brigade, commanded by Hon. Stanley Mathews.

The author having promised many of his former comrades, on taking leave of them when the regiment disbanded, to publish this work, has this apology to offer for the long delay in placing the work before the public: First—For several years immediately succeeding the rebellion, the country was flooded with wild, romantic and fictitious story books of the sanguinary struggle, written principally by men and women whose sources of information were vague newspaper reports, lavishly colored by their own fruitful imaginations, causing the reading public to tire of literature relating to the late war. Second—The author's unsettled affairs, in making a new home in the West; and, thirdly, the scattered condition of the survivors, making it difficult to obtain from brother officers certain statistical matters material to the work.

Hoping the true and moral character of this work, free from any of that bitter sectional feeling usually found in such books, will make the following pages a welcome and interesting visitor in every home, and especially to all old soldiers and their numerous friends.

THE AUTHOR.

CONTENTS.

HISTORY EIGHTH KENTUCKY.

CHAPTER I.

The Clouds of War. Kentucky's Neutrality. Union Home Guards. Invasion. Enlisting. Recruits Arming themselves with Rifles and Shot guns. Rendezvousing at Estill Springs. Awkward Drilling. Organizing the Regiment. Flag Presentation by Loyal Ladies. Response of the Eighth.

CHAPTER II.

Marching Orders. Taking Leave of Friends. A Rainy March. Loyalty in Richmond, Ky. A Snow Storm. Officers Paying for Chickens. Arrive at Lebanon. Putting on Style. Drilling. Serious Sickness. Moving Camp and Making Beds. Married Soldiers Desirous to be Furloughed. A Shrewd Woman and a Sharp Lieutenant. Kindness of Citizens. Our Death Roll Increases. Pay Day. Marching to Louisville. Boat Ride. An Indignant Boat Crew. Excited Negroes.

CHAPTER III.

A Silent Southern City. Buell's Unpleasant Orders. Cutting Rebels' Timber. Moving South. Wading Stone River. Heavy Camp and Picket Duty. Ward fools the Doctor and is caught. Shooting a Rebel fool. Pig Skins. The Eighth at Wartrace. Catching a Rebel Surgeon. Fortifying. Cutting Railroad Timbers and Guarding Bridges. On the Mountains under Gen. Dumont. Hard Living. Returning to Camp at Wartrace. A detail wash "Dobins" neck. Fourth of July.

CHAPTER IV.

Night Ride to Elk River Bridge. Marching in a Rain Storm. A Knapsack Squabble. Fortifying Tullahoma. The 35th Indiana joins the Brigade. Picketing and Foraging. March to Murfreesboro. Putting the Darkies to Digging Rifle-pits. A silent Night Move ends in Hard Marching. Nelson expecting Attack at Murfreesboro. A hot March to McMinnville. Morgan Evacuates. Expedition over Cany Fork. A hard set of Teamsters. Rain. Hard work, wet clothes and no grub. Counter-march. Green Apples. Nelson's Drills. Expedition to Liberty. Nelson and the pie vender. "Thirty-fives" run a Distillery.

CHAPTER V.

Loyalty leaving McMinnville. March back to Murfreesboro. Scarcity of Greenbacks. An Accommodating Sutler. Troops passing through Nashville. On to Kentucky. Pants only for the ragged Gray-backs in camp. Leaving Tennessee with full Stomachs. The Flag and Loyalty in Kentucky. Branson and the Goat. On half Rations. Grating Corn Hard Marching. Drinking Mule Soup. Skirmishing ahead. Arrive at Cave City. Novel Cooking. Wormy Flour. Soldiers Distrusting Buell. Sleeping with wet garments. A Race for the Ohio. Famishing with Thirst. Midnight Entrance into Louisville. Condition of the Troops.

CHAPTER VI.

Expecting Pay, but Double-quick after the Johnnies. Skirmishing. Scarcity of Water. Battle of Perryville. Rebels Retreating. Indignant Kentucky Soldiers. Hunting a fight at Danville. On toward Crab Orchard. Night attack on the Johnnies. They leave a hot Breakfast. Rebels Blockading the Road near Wildcat. The 8th Surprise and Capture a Camp of Rebel Recruits. On to Somerset. Early Snow. March to Columbus. Sad Reports from Home. The 8th and 21st desire a few Greenbacks. Married Men wanting Furloughs. Pay day at Glasgow. Moving on to Tennessee. A big day's Washing at Galatin.

CHAPTER VII.

Slipping on to Morgan at Lebanon. Heavy Rations of Flour, Bacon and Whisky. A novel Supply Train. Foraging at Silver Springs. Guarding Supplies to Rural Hill. Attack at Breakfast. Discomfitted Rebels leave seven dead. Wiseman tumbling a "Jip." Col. Hawkins Compliments the Eighth. Camp nearer Nashville. Changes in the Command. Move to the Murfreesboro Pike. Rosecrans Inspects the Army. Foraging and Battle at Dobins' Ferry. Our Dead and Wounded. Another move. After Absentees in Louisville

CHAPTER VIII.

The Army moves on the Enemy. The Eighth's Company Commanders. Skirmishing in the rain. A Sunday in Bivouac. Pickets' Armistice. Arrival at Stone River. Two Armies Facing. Heavy Skirmishing. Terrible Battle the last day of 1862. Wading cold water. Third Brigade a Bait to Rosy's Trap. Magnificent War Picture. A gallant Resistance by the Third Brigade. Breckenridge falls into the trap. Terrible Slaughter. Murfreesboro ours. Burying Dead. Bad Weather. Loss of Comrades. Irishman's Notion of Putting Down Rebels.

CHAPTER IX.

Torn Battle Flags in Kentucky Legislature. A Hospital Town. Picketing and practicing Economy. Death of three gallant Officers. Foraging on a large scale. A Rebel dislikes his Voucher. Fortifying M. The Status of the Slaves discussed. More Deaths from Wounds. Guarding Pontoons. On a Reconnoissance. Rain, mud and songs. Camp on Lytle's Creek. A stylish Inspector Wets his Pants. Off to Snow Hill with one hundred rounds. Charging the Enemy. Victory. Return to Camp.

CHAPTER X.

Heavy Drills and Picket Duty. Col. Matthews' Farewell. A Mammoth "Nigger" Dance causes Alarm. Maj. Broadhus' and Col. May's Departure. Capt. Mayhew and Adjt. Clark Promoted. Officers being Married to Commissions. Marking Comrades' Graves. Swap for Enfield Rifles. Smith's Gun the Brightest. Dobin Spikes tries Bean Juice. Witnessing the Shooting of a Deserter. Army moves Forward. Marching and Scouting. Union Songs and Rebel Hate. At Woodbury. At McMinnville again. Ornamenting Camp. Unwelcome Harvesters. The last Man ever Tied up.

CHAPTER XI.

Over the Mountains. Topography of Sequatchie. Rattlesnakes. Pikeville. Brains Hockersmith and the Rebel Beauty. Living on Produce. The Loyal Refugee Preacher. A good Work begins. Down the Valley. Crossing the Tennessee. Wet Men. Guarding Supply Train. A piled up Country. Passing the Gate City. Three Miles of Fight. Entering Ringold, Ga. Frightened Women. Back to Gordon's Mills and McLamore's Cave. A Sweet Incense of Frying Mutton.

CHAPTER XII.

Reconnoitering and Skirmishing at Chicamauga. A Cold Night and Piteous Cries of the Wounded. Description of the Two Days' Battle. Gallant Charge by the 51st Ohio and 8th Kentucky. Return to the city, war worn and brush torn. Loss of Comrades.

CHAPTER XIII.

Siege of Chattanooga. Digging Day and Night. Under Fire. On Quarter Rations. Picket Repartee. Another Picture of War. Religious Worship. Frank Captures Rebel Beeves. Rosecrans and Crittenden Farewell. The Command Changed to the 4th Corps. A Detail of the Brigade at Field Hospital. Forage for a Living. At Moccasin Point. Wauhatchie and Shell Mound. Dilapidated Clothing. Building Winter Quarters.

CHAPTER XIV.

Over Bad Roads with three days' Rations and Sixty Rounds. Facing Frowning Lookout. Pile Knapsacks and Climbing. Surprising the Enemy in day-light. A Rich Harvest of Prisoners. Novel Missiles. Ward Silencing a Sharpshooter. Battle above the Clouds. Carrying the Flag on Point Lookout. Capturing Camp and Commissaries. An exciting Battle Scene. Finishing Winter Quarters. Consolidation of the Regiment at Shell Mound Parting with Brother Officers. Maj. Clark's Farewell.

CHAPTER XV.

Re-enlisting. Manner of Doubling Companies. Leaving the "Illegant" Shanties. Incidents of the March to Cleveland, Tenn. Self Reliance of the Soldiers. Form new Camp and Acquaintances. Veterans get Pay, and an Expedition to Buzzard's Roost. In Leaky Tents at Blue Springs. A Rainy March and Miserable Night Ride. A Supperless Set. Camp at Chattanooga. Chuck-a-luckers Burying Mules. Snow-balling. Veterans Dressing up. An Officer's Advice to his Men.

CHAPTER XVI.

Veterans take a Thirty Days' Furlough. Soldiers' Home. In Louisville. Leaving Lexington. Cleaning out a Hotel. Good Behavior. Home and Friends. How a Southern

Rights Woman became Union. Returning to the War. A Reinstated Cook. Garrison and Picket Duties around the "Gate City." Some Characteristic Citizens. Afraid of a Yankee Gun. A sad case of Sudden Poverty.

CHAPTER XVII.

Guarding Trains Front and Rear. A hard lot of Bounty Jumpers. The Fourth of July. Steadman's hard Orders to Citizens. Rebel Raid on Dalton increases our Duty. A Hot Valley. Fanciful Reverie of a Thunder Storm. Soldiers taking Interest in Religion and Politics. A Characteristic Debate. Model Worship. Forest's Raid on our Cracker Line. Platform Cars to Cumberland Tunnel. Waiting for Attack at Block Houses.

CHAPTER XVIII.

Life Twenty Days at Elk River. A Destitute Country. An Impressive Funeral. Night Ride to Bridgeport. Returning to Chattanooga. Picketing with Colored Troops. New Clothing. Arrival of the Fourth Corps. A Camp of Discouraged Atlanta Citizens. The Eighth sent to Reseca and Calhoun. Turning over Government Property. Making Muster out Rolls. Bidding good-bye to Lieut. Pucket and the Veterans. All aboard for Nashville. Receiving Pay at Louisville. Disbanding.

CHAPTER XIX.

Appendix.

HISTORY

OF THE

Eighth Kentucky Volunteers.

CHAPTER I.

In the month of December, 1860, the State of South Carolina passed the rash and fatal Ordinance of Secession. This dark, ominous cloud of civil discord that arose in the South and gathered strength and blackness as it rolled northward, threatening soon to burst in a terrific storm of civil war, blood and carnage, and convulse this mighty Government from center to circumference—a war that was soon to stain hundreds of battlefields with the blood of many thousands of brave and good men from every part of our glorious Union. Early in the winter of 1861 all classes of our citizens in Central Kentucky became intensely interested in the question of the propriety of Kentucky's seceding and casting her fortune with the other Slave States, which had been, by excitement and forced elections, hurled out of the Union into the so called Southern Confederacy, where slavery instead of freedom was to become the chief corner-stone of this new national edifice.

In Central Kentucky, and especially in those counties bordering on the southern part of the "Bluegrass region," debates became decidedly warm and spirited. A small majority of the best citizens immediately took a firm and decided stand against secession and rebellion, while many whose love for the "divine" institution of African slavery assumed that peculiar cloak for treason called neutrality, and loudly demanded compromises instead of coercion ; and many were from the first rebels at heart, who openly proclaimed on the streets of our towns their wicked and treasonable designs to destroy or divide this Union of States.

The winter passed. The mad fire of secession continued to rage. Active preparations for war were carried on in the seceded States. Union men were astonished at the inactivity of Buchanan's weak Administration ; while rebels rejoiced and exulted over the surrender of that brave and good man, Major Anderson, and his gallant little band of heroes at Fort Sumter. Rebel companies were drilling in Central and Southern Kentucky, and open, outspoken Union men were threatened with hanging or banishment. We began to think the time had come when we should rub up our old shot-guns and trusty rifles, and instead of discussing secession meetings were called to consult as to the best methods of self-protection.

The legerdemain by which the extreme Southern States were juggled out of the Union had so far proved a success. Only let it be granted that where thirteen or more parties have entered into a solemn contract with each other either of the parties can rightfully withdraw from the arrangement when he pleases without the consent of the others, and you can prove anything. Any man whose mind can be taught that, could be made believe anything, and the Southern people were carefully taught to believe it. They contended that while the States which chose to secede could not be rightfully coerced to remain in the Union, those States which chose to remain must be forced to secede. But the Confederate logicians in Kentucky hatched a new lie called neutrality, and declared that Kentucky should be neutral until the rebellion should become strong enough to swallow her at a mouthful. Governor Magoffin, whose sympathies were strong for the South, issued a proclamation calling for the organization of the State Militia, and also convening the Legislature to consider the crisis. The 22d of May, 1861, the Senate passed a resolution declaring "that Kentucky will never sever her connection with the National Government, nor take up arms for either belligerent." This resolution was lost in the House of Representatives by a large vote. The secessionists of Kentucky began to be alarmed, and their fears were not diminished when the result of the election held the first of July showed a majority for the Union candidates of more than fifty-five thousand votes ; and

Kentucky Union men began to take courage at the action of the President, and the hearty response by troops from the Northern States to his call for 75,000 three-months' men to meet the rebel army then gathered in Northeastern Virginia. And many believed the "sectional troubles" would soon blow over without the loss of much blood. Union home guards were organized in most counties along the Kentucky River and throughout the north part of the State—probably the best move that could have been made at that time. But, as subsequent events proved, to have attempted to put down the rebellion with home guards and three months' men was about as wise as to try to put out the flames of a burning building with a squirt-gun. The writer had the honor to command one of these home guard companies in Estill County. We met twice a week, every man with rifle or shot-gun ready for any emergency, but principally to drill. The military display and general awkwardness of both rank and file on these occasions would have excited the profanity of a West Point general. But we had the best of raw material of which to make soldiers. These undisciplined companies contained brave and fearless men, accustomed to handling firearms from early boyhood. They were excellent marksmen, and only needed schooling and discipline to make them what most of them afterward proved, the best of soldiers.

Before the first of August, 1861, so many of these home guards were organized throughout the country, those would-be Confederate soldiers who had begun to drill and bluster in our midst, began to think it would be more healthy a little further south, and in their attempt to join Zollicoffer's forces (then invading the State) many were gobbled up as prisoners by these undisciplined home guards, among them James B. Clay, son of the great statesman, who, with a large number of followers, were sent under guard to Louisville. Most of them took the oath of loyalty and were released. This invading army of rebels caused many of us to doubt the efficiency of our home organizations, lacking combined co-operation and discipline.

In August, 1861, Sidney M. Barnes, a lawyer gifted with more than ordinary talent as a speaker, and proprietor of the noted watering place "Estill Springs," near Irvine, Ky., addressed the citizens of Madison, Estill and some of the adjoining counties, at a series of meetings, principally held at the times and places where the home guards met to drill. He ably pointed out the many disadvantages under which we would labor, and the danger of the State being overrun by the rebel army, the necessity of being armed with guns of the same caliber, of uniform clothing, and of a more perfect organization, with some assurance of remuneration for our services. The Colonel humorously remarked: "Notwithstanding your bravery, which is undoubted, should the rebel army succeed in advancing this far, all you married men in the home guards will be sure to want to go home and see after Sally and the children."

On the 14th of September, 1861, a battalion muster of half a score of home guard companies met at Texas, in Madison County. The loyal citizens of the surrounding country came with well-filled baskets of the choicest provisions the country could afford. A picnic of mammoth proportions was the result to which everybody was welcomed by the loyal, kind hearted women, who formed a large part of the great throng of people. Captains Powell and Wilson, who had partially formed two companies of three years' volunteers, were present with their new recruits beating up for volunteers, and no less than four other parts of companies were represented by as many flags, followed by drums and fife, appealing to the patriotism of the young men to take arms in defense of the best Government ever vouchsafed to man on earth. There are many survivors of the Eighth that dated their enrollment from that bright 14th of September, 1861, and became members of Companies B, C and H. The two former companies, under Powell and Wilson, had obtained their full quotas by the 22d, and on that day were given a bountiful feast by the good, old, loyal fathers and mothers of Station Camp, in Estill County, as a farewell token of their love to the "boys" and devotion to the cause of union and liberty. That long table extending half across Uncle Eb. Wilson's pasture, loaded with rich and savory food, surrounded by kind mothers, sisters and sweethearts, insisting on us partaking of more when we had eat to repletion, was a scene and pleasure we often recalled to mind when on quarter rations "Away down south in Dixie." These two companies rendezvoused the 23d at Estill Springs, carrying with them many good shot-guns and rifles "borrowed" from reluctant rebel owners. The new encampment was armed principally by "loaned guns" of all kinds and calibers.

The 26th September, Capt. R. Winbourn and myself left Estill Springs on a recruiting tour, each of us taking different routes, he going up the Kentucky River into Owsley County, and myself with a few recruits rode to the farm of Mr. Wills, where our first appointment to beat up for volunteers had been previously announced. The surrounding hills re-echoed the sound of our martial band, the music of which was not of the best, but the patriotic ardor being augmented by the rumored invasion of the State by the rebels under Zollicoffer, caused men, women and children to collect from all directions, some bearing large baskets filled with provisions, all with hearts full of love for our old flag and freedom. At 10 o'clock a. m. several hundreds of eager, expectant persons had assembled. The poor music was followed by an equally poor speech from the writer, and this was followed by loud and boisterous cheering. We hoisted our flag, headed by our three amateur musicians, playing their one and only tune, "Sally is the gal for me." As each recruit fell into the moving line loud cheers rent the air. In a short time we had about eighteen recruits, among them the brave and lamented Lieut. W. B. Cox, who gave his life's blood as a sacrifice for human liberty on the battle-field of Stone River. After partaking of a bountiful dinner, *a la* pic nic, we agreed to meet within two days, the 28th, at one Mr. Berryman's, where the bad speaking and music were again followed by a call for recruits. Several handsome young women took the flag and marched after the music, appealing to the young men to fall in and go fight for the best government on earth. These appeals were not in vain, as one boy said "none but traitors or cowards could stand back now." Nor did the tearful, pleading eyes of fond and affectionate wives restrain husbands from enlisting. Here our numbers were increased to upwards of thirty. According to instructions from Col. Barnes, we proceeded to collect a sufficient number of guns from rebels and rebel sympathizers to arm each new recruit. Many laughable incidents occurred in thus collecting arms. I will recite only one of the many: One T——, near the Spout Spring, had openly and publicly swore that " no Lincolnite should ever take his rifle to Estill Springs unless he first received the one charge it contained. Knowing the truth of the old saying that "a barking dog doesn't bite," I went alone to his cabin door and demanded the loan of his gun. He first denied having one—with trembling limbs and husky voice he declared his brother in Clark had it. When told that was "too thin," and that no fooling would be permitted, he acknowledged that it was behind a wide board over the door, and told me to take it down, which I declined to do, telling him of his previous threat, and to hand it to me himself. This he did. With tears in his eyes he said, "Capt., take care of her, fur she cost me twenty-five dollars, and I split rails at fifty cents a hundred to pay most ov it." He was told if he conducted himself as a good, loyal citizen, he would receive his gun again. In justice to many of these men of whom guns were taken, be it said that they, like Mr. T——, proved to become Union men, and regained their reluctantly loaned property.

On the 3d October, in company with Lieut. Cox and twenty more of the recruits, we returned to Estill Springs, and were sworn into the U. S. service for three years or during the war, unless sooner discharged by proper authority.

Recruiting parties with squads were daily arriving. The Colonel's long rows of neat cottage buildings were full, and a large quantity of lumber procured to build quarters. We were bountifully supplied with excellent beef and bacon. The services of an experienced baker was secured, who furnished us good bread, full rations of coffee and sugar, and often a wagon load of potatoes were dumped into camp as a donation from some good old farmer. But the insufficient number of skillets, frying-pans and coffee pots, promiscuously gathered up and brought in by thoughtful recruits, and the great number of self-appointed, inexperienced cooks, caused confusion and no little discord. To avoid this a certain number of cooks were selected for each company or part of company, to attend to culinary affairs alone. After this judicious arrangement we lived well for soldiers, and many of those company cooks were there given "nick names" that they carried throughout the war. One Harris, of Company H, for his scrupulous cleanliness and dexterity in handling the dish-cloth, received the affectionate name of "mother." I. Ward, Company F, kindly answered to the name of "Aunt Sally," &c.

The 4th October, Capt. Jamison arrived with a full company from about the three forks of the Kentucky River. A few days later, Capt. Winbourn with another squad arrived and joined us, thus augmenting our company, H, to about sixty. Lieut. C. Benton soon after came in with a large squad, that subsequently became Company E. By the 18th October there were no less than fifteen parts of companies and full companies in camp. Col. Barnes informed us that companies could have only until the 10th November to complete their organizations. Then considerable splicing of squads took place, and parts of squads bolting to other parts of companies, the men not being pleased with the selfish arrangements their recognized leaders were trying to make with others, securing to themselves a lieutenantcy, and making no provision for even a non-commissioned officer for any of their devoted followers. Thus men were, after being sworn in, allowed to leave any company not full and join what company he chose, and then have a choice in the selection of company officers, even down to 8th corporal.

The 23d October our encampment was thrown into

a furor of excitement on the receipt of the news of Gen. Zollicoffer and his rebel horde being defeated in the spirited little fight at Wild Cat Mountain, by a few regiments of Indianians and a few raw Kentucky recruits. About the 28th October, Captains Mayhew, McDaniel and J. B. Banton's companies from Barbourville and Manchester arrived at the Springs. Our reception of this important addition to our command was enthusiastically warm and noisy. These companies had smelt powder at Wild Cat, and we met them in the town of Irvine with music and much cheering, and escorted them as conquering heroes to our camp.

The measles had broken out among us, and notwithstanding good medical aid was secured, several hundred of the 8th boys went through this sickening contagion. Though none died immediately from the disease, it no doubt subsequently caused the death of a large number.

Several hours each day was spent in an awkward attempt at drill. Progress was unavoidably slow, as nearly all the self-appointed officers and drill sergeants were as little skilled in tactics as the men, who found it difficult to habituate themselves to being disciplined by such awkward superiors. Lieutenant-Colonel May, Major G. B. Broadhus and Captain Powell had served in the Mexican war as Lieutenants, and Captain R. B. Hickman had attended a military school a few months previous to joining the Eighth. All the other officers were novices in tactics and regulations.

From the 1st to the 10th of November the principal excitement in camp was the splicing of squads into companies and the election of officers. With so much electioneering, discipline existed only in name. Some exciting and uncomfortably close races, but the best of humor prevailed, defeated aspirants cheerfully acquiescing in the choice of the majority.

The 13th November, ten companies being organized, with maximum number, making an aggregate of a few over nine hundred. The newly elected company officers met and decided upon the letter and rank of each company, as follows:

Co. A—Captain, J. D. Mayhew.
    1st Lieut., Wm. Ketchen.
Co. B—Captain, A. D. Powell.
    1st Lieut., I. Neal.
    2d Lieut., J. Blackwell.
Co. C—Captain, John Wilson.
    1st Lieut., Wm. Park.
    2d Lieut., Cassius Park.
Co. D—Captain, R. B. Jamison.
    1st Lieut., J. P. Gumm.
    2d Lieut., T. Carson.
Co. E—Captain, R. B. Hickman.
    1st Lieut., C. D. Benton.
    2d Lieut., Perry Nickolls.
Co. F—Captain, John B. Banton.
    1st Lieut.. Barton Dixon.
    2d Lieut., Newton Hughes.
Co. G—Captain, L. C. Minter.

1st Lieut., Caleb Hughes.
2d Lieut., Winfield S. Spencer.
Co. H—Captain, Rhodes Winbourn.
1st Lieut., Wade B. Cox.
2d Lieut., T. J. Wright.
Co. I—Captain, Wm. McDaniel.
1st Lieut., ——Crooks.
2d Lieut., ——Amy.
Co. K—Captain, Henry Thomas.
1st Lieut., Wesley Stewart.
2d Lieut., Wm. Smallwood.

Col. S. M. Barnes chosen Colonel; Reuben May, of Clay county, Lieut. Colonel; Green B. Broadhus, of Madison, Major; John S. Clark, of Irvine, Adjutant, and Timothy Paul, of Clay, Chaplain.

Three days after, we received an entire outfit of camp and garrison equipage, except tents. The arms were the old altered muskets. With our new clothing the Eighth began to assume quite a martial appearance, and the officers were becoming indefatigable in study and drill.

By the 26th November the majority of our measles-stricken comrades had become convalescent. About this time the Colonel received orders from General Thomas to break up camp and march to Lebanon. The evening of the 27th November a delegation of loyal ladies from the town of Irvine and vicinity assembled on the long veranda of the principal Springs building, one of them bearing above her a large and beautiful silk flag, made by them expressly for gift to the Eighth Kentucky.

The regiment formed dress parade, though the officers' uniforms were as varied as the habiliments of any thirty or forty citizens usually are. The proper salutation had to be made with the hand, as none of us had purchased swords or uniforms. We closed column by division, when Joseph Clark, Jr., made the presentation speech for the ladies, winding up with the admonition to "Carry that flag to victory; never let it be deserted or dishonored by brave Kentuckians!" The throbbing hearts and quivering lips of our brave mountain boys responded, "Never!" "Never!" then gave three cheers for the loyal ladies of old Estill.

CHAPTER II.

The morning of the 28th November, long before the light of day made its appearance, the echoes from "Sweet Lick Nob" resounded the music from our drums. Instantly all became astir. Much bluster, loud talking and hasty cooking, mixed with considerable profanity, was indulged in, something not unusual with new troops preparing to march. Acting Quartermaster Curtis had procured the services of a few citizens with teams and wagons for this especial march. About sunrise the regiment formed, amid music and some cheering. Every man appeared eager to be moving, as if the suppression of the rebellion mainly depended on their individual exertions. Many of those scarcely recovered from measles were in the ranks with well-filled knapsacks, arms and accoutrements buckled on, scorning to be left behind. Many were bidding hasty farewells to near and dear friends, not thinking it would be the last with ah, so many manly, ruddy boys, in the bloom of youth. Some time was spent in ferrying the command over the Kentucky River, at White's Ferry, where many good, old loyal fathers and tearful mothers and sisters had collected to take, perhaps, the last look at son or brother.

> "'Neath war's dark clouds, the sturdy volunteer,
> By Freedom taught, his country to revere;
> Bids home and friends a hasty, sad adieu,
> And treads where dangers all his steps pursue."

The threatening clouds began to shed their torrents of water on us about ten o'clock a. m., and continued to pour all day. The road, principally a mud pike, soon became a loblolly of mud and water. At four p. m. we entered Richmond, Ky. The loyal citizens there, not only welcomed us to the spacious Court House and two large churches, but gratuitously furnished victuals to both men and officers.

The 29th the rain continued to fall. Every soldier who drank whisky was allowed to purchase his canteen full before starting on the march, to counteract the unhealthy effects of the inclement weather. This well-meant kindness on the part of the Colonel and some other officers proved in most cases an injury to the men, as quite a number through the day used this precautionary beverage too freely while marching the thirteen miles on the Lancaster Pike. We camped near Miller's Mills, and soon had the Woodland pasture of T. Burnham dotted with blazing log fires, drying our thoroughly soaked raiments. The wagons containing our Company tents met us here. The rain ceased and the thermometer went down very fast. Tents were pitched amidst a first-class snow-storm. Here we eat our first "hard-tack." The commissioned officers held a consultation and chose from among several aspirants T. Burnham as Quartermaster, and he was soon after commissioned. The morning of the 30th, Colonel B —— did considerable swearing at some of the men, whose whisky had proved a hindrance to their alacrity in loading camp and garrison equipage. That evening, the 8th, we marched through Lancaster, county seat of Gerrard County, and camped within one and a half miles of that place. A good supply of straw made our tents quite comfortable. After dark a disturbance among Mr. Robinson's chickens caused the Colonel to detail a guard, as the boys said to prevent the minks from feasting on poultry. The first day of December we passed through Danville and encamped within two miles of town. Before dark a report was circulated through camp that the citizens of that vicinity were rebel sympathizers, consequently next morning the ground about camp was covered with feathers and occasionally spots of hog hair, indicating that the men had devoured the poultry and made a fair beginning on pork. In justice to the neighborhood I will state that we afterward learned that the people were generally good Union citizens, and proved it by their conduct toward us the next October, after the rebels had been eating their chickens.

Snow began to fall early the 2d, and before we halted in camp, in the neighborhood of Perryville, five or six inches of snow covered the earth. We suffered much with cold feet and fingers in pitching tents and building fires. The following morning the company officers, upon learning that old Mr. Bloomfield was a staunch Unionist, made up money and paid him for the chickens that had found their way into camp from his premises.

The 3d day of December ended our first march. On arriving within one and a half miles of Lebanon we were met by Colonel Fry, in command of the Fourth Kentucky, with colors and music. We were conducted to a piece of woodland, south of the Danville Pike, near the quarters of the latter regiment. The deep snow was scraped away, and tents erected in regular order. Marquees were issued to the officers, two to a company. The next day the men were organized into messes of eight men each. Officers' messes were also established, with regular cooks. Thus we began to live quite in military style. The officers' commissary bills were light. The men drew more rations than they could consume, but instead of this surplus being accounted for as company savings, the men cheerfully gave it to their Captains and Lieutenants. But the reader will remember that the science of war has to be learned before it is practised. We remained here at "Camp Swamp" seventeen days, drilling vigorously whenever the weather would permit. About ten days after our arrival here some of the men began to sicken with a kind of fever—afterward called camp fever—which proved fatal to many of the Eighth during the winter, especially those who had recently recovered from the measles. Our first death occurred the 18th—Granville Lady, Company C. We buried him according to regulations. The convalescents arrived from Irvine the 15th, the men continuing to increase the sick list. Colonel Barnes decided to move camp to a higher and dryer place.

The 20th we moved camp half mile east of Lebanon, and pitched tents in Spaulding's apple orchard—a high piece of ground, but unprotected from the cold winds. Our Quartermaster appeared to experience much difficulty in procuring sufficient straw for bedding. The few teams of citizens which came from Estill County with the regiment were kept busy all day in transferring the camp and garrison. A large number of the men were sick, and the company officers began to look more closely after the health and comfort of the men. Details were sent into adjacent cornfields to gather dead grass. Captain Powell gave Company B permission to take hay from a stack near camp, but Colonel Barnes soon stopped them, when the Captain and the Colonel indulged in some short words about unauthorized and promiscuous foraging. The men gathered up old boards and placed under the straw on the ground for bunks. Neither surgeons, officers nor men appeared to realize the importance of having the bunks raised off the ground, where the straw soon absorbed moisture enough to kill a healthy man in two weeks. But the line officers were anxious to do all they could for their men, and money was made up by them and sheet-iron stoves purchased for each tent. Still the sickness increased at a fearful rate.

The last of December our Quartermaster received our transportation outfit—twelve old army wagons and a number of unbroke mules. Our newly-appointed teamsters had some lively times drilling their awkward squads of drafted four-footed recruits. Hauling our daily supply of wood gave them an excellent opportunity to practice the "Mule in the mud."

As the Christmas holidays approached a number of married men of the Eighth began to importune Colonel Barnes for furloughs to visit their families. Some had enlisted only a few days before the regiment marched from Estill Springs, and had left their domestic affairs in a very bad condition. But the wise old Colonel well knew that if he granted the married men leave of absence the boys would urgently plead to be allowed to go home to see their intended wives, and as it was impossible to furlough all, none were granted. As we had not yet been mustered into the United States service, a good many believed they would risk the terrors of a court martial, and on the morning of the 26th several members of Companies H and F failed to put in an appearance at roll-call. A few days after Lieutenant Cox, of Company H, proceeded to Madison and Estill Counties with orders to bring back the absentees. Several amusing incidents occurred while the Lieutenant was collecting these fond husbands, who afterward proved to be the best and bravest of soldiers.

Isaac T——, the father of several children and the husband of a good-looking, shrewd woman, was supposed to be enjoying the company of his family during this snowy Christmas night. The Lieutenant cautiously approached the now happy home of the T——s. A vigilant watch-dog warned the family of the approach of an intruder. A rap on the door, followed by the inquiry if Mr. T—— was at home, brought the response from a feminine voice within: "Oh, no sir! he's in Mr. Barnes' regiment." After some parleying the Lieutenant was permitted to enter and warm himself. He then began diligent search to see if any lurking husband could be found about the premises. At last the Lieutenant said he was very sorry to have disturbed the lady, and turning to the bed recently occupied by the woman, in which lay a small sleeping specimen of the T—— family, he tenderly lifted the little white-headed infant out, and turning toward Mrs. T——, said: "You will please take this child." "Oh, sir, I pray you let the dear, sick child lay!" The Lieutenant insisted, and she reluctantly relieved him of the precious charge. Then he lifted off the nice feather bed, and behold there lay the missing Isaac, who crawled out laughing, acknowledged that the Lieutenant had outwitted his wife, terminated his "French" furlough, and broke up the happiness of his holidays at home; though not until that cheerful but defeated woman had prepared a hot supper, which Lieutenant Cox and her husband enjoyed together before starting on their return to Lebanon.

The new year of 1862 began with a warm rain, and the remaining winter months were exceptionally wet and muddy. The number of our sick increased alarmingly. Dr. John Mills began to find a regimental surgeon's position quite a responsible one. He not only had two churches full of sick, but a large number were at private houses in town, where they received the best of treatment at the hands of the loyal men and women of the place. In many instances they not only allowed our sick boys shelter, but prepared suitable food with their own hands, and doubtless saved the lives of many of the survivors of the Eighth Kentucky. The author, among many others, will never in life forget the kindness of Dr. Mudd, Mr. and Mrs. Speed, Mrs. Milbourn and Mr. Philips, with a host of others. The Misses Selby, though strong "Southern Rights" women, owners of a large hotel, gave up some of their rooms to our sick, and were very kind to those quartered in the Selby House. These old maids were untiring in their care for Captain Minter, and probably saved his life, as his doctors said nothing but their nursing could have returned to us one of our best young officers, who subsequently lost his life in action at Stone River. Notwithstanding the good citizens of Lebanon and the well portion of the regiment did all they could for our sick, with the attention of several resident physicians, deaths through the latter part of January and first half of February were of almost daily occurrence.

The 15th of January, by laborious work with us inexperienced officers, we had our muster-in rolls prepared, and were that day mustered into the United States service for three years or during the war.

Captain Mayhew, with Company A, returned from the Rolling Fork of Salt River, about eight miles distant from Lebanon, where he had been two weeks guarding a bridge, Buckner's rebs, who had made their appearance there and committed some depredations on private individuals, having fallen back toward Bowling Green, where the enemy was said to be in large force.

The 21st January we received the welcome news of the defeat of the rebels at Mill Springs, Ky., and the death of their General, Zollicoffer, and his Adjutant-General, Payton, by our forces under General Thomas. We made many demonstrations of joy over this great victory, as it was called at the time. We did not then know that such a battle was a mere skirmish compared to some of the bloody engagements some of us would participate in before the rebellion would be whipped into peace. But as anxious as we were to see such a result, we did not desire that other troops should gain all the honor and victories, therefore we were very desirous to leave Lebanon and be in more active service.

The Fourteenth Kentucky Infantry and the First Kentucky Cavalry had, in December, taken an active part under Colonel Garfield in routing Marshal and his rebel horde out of Southeast Kentucky. Now, the Fourth Kentucky, which contained many of our neighbor boys, had been winning bright laurels at Mill Springs, while here we were guarding a few quartermaster stores, nursing our sick, and burying our deceased comrades in numbers almost as great as were slain on our side in gaining this much talked-of victory at Mill Springs. The continuous rains and consequent mud prevented drilling what few men were able for duty, and most of them were daily on duty as guards, nurses, or haulers of wood and other fatigue duty.

About the first of February we moved our camp down near the depot, and remained there doing garrison duty until the 10th of March. Before this Forts Henry and Donaldson had fallen into our comrades' hands, Bowling Green had been evacuated without any serious engagement, and Kentucky was nearly cleared of armed bodies of the enemy. We daily chafed at our being held back.

The 7th of March the Eighth was paid up to the 31st December, 1861, having previously received one month's pay from the State. Two of our line officers, Lieutenants Crook and Amy, had resigned, and during the winter forty-three of our men had died, three times that number were yet unable to leave their beds, with about 250 convalescents, most of them quite feeble.

On the 9th Colonel Barnes called the company officers together and informed them that we would march toward Louisville the next morning. Our men, sick and well, received this order with enthusiastic cheers. The remainder of the day was a busy time with rank and file. Many had debts to settle with citizens, others letters to write home informing dear friends that at last we were "bound for Dixie." Captains Hickman and Winbourn, Lieutenants Nickols, Martin and Carson, being reported unable for duty, were ordered to take charge of the convalescents able to leave the hospitals and private houses, where many were quartered, and follow in a few days on the cars to Louisville and join the regiment there.

On the morning of the 10th of March, 1862, the camp of the 8th Kentucky was all life, everybody hurrying his comrade in loading up our garrison equipage. A cold, misty rain was falling. At last all the good byes had been said to our kind Lebanon friends, and the column marched out the Louisville pike. Having learned by sad experience not to let men just out of sick beds to unnecessarily expose themselves, our column did not cover half the space it did when we left Estill Springs. The rain continued to drizzle, and the limestone road became quite sloppy. At four o'clock p. m., we halted in Springfield, the county seat of Washington, and quartered the men in the court house. Company commanders borrowed several cook stoves of citizens, and the men soon had the town perfumed with frying bacon and boiling coffee. The 11th we camped near Bardstown. Here Col. Barnes informed us he had just learned that we were brigaded with the 23d Kentucky, Col. Munday, and the 3d Minnesota, Col. Lester, and that he had orders to march directly to Louisville, and probably thence to Tennessee. We passed through Bardstown the 12th, with our colors unfurled, keeping step to the lively music of our martial band. That night we procured abundance of straw for bedding, and the owner of the pasture being a home rebel, talked loudly of private rights, until Maj. Broadhus told him if he said another word he would arrest him and march him to Louisville before a musket. The 13th we pitched our tents at Hays Springs, on the bluffs of Salt River, where we also found the 23d Kentucky. During the night and next morning a heavy rain fell, making the cooking a difficult task, and marching very disagreeable. Col. Barnes proceeded to Louisville in company with Col. Munday.

The night of the 14th we camped within three miles of the city, where we remained several days. The 15th our sick and convalescent arrived at the depot. The officers not knowing where to find the regiment, quartered the men in barracks, where they remained several days. When those able to join the regiment reported they appeared proud to once more take their arms and places in the ranks with their comrades. All the men not able to march were given descriptive rolls and sent to the hospitals in the city, principally to No. 7.

We exchanged our old army wagons for new ones, cleaned up our guns, prepared five days' cooked rations, and early the morning of the 19th struck tents, and, during the prevalence of a heavy rain storm, marched through the city to the wharf, where the remainder of the day was spent in transferring our camp and garrison equipage, including mules, wagons and horses, to two steamers, the "Nashville" and "Lady Jackson." The Twenty-third Kentucky was assigned to the "Jacob Strader," and the Third Minnesota, Colonel Lester commanding, to the "Undine" and the "Denmark." Captain Rice, of the Third Minnesota, once a citizen of

Estill County, and an old personal and political enemy of Colonel Barnes, met the latter on the wharf. The Captain extended his hand, saying, "Colonel Barnes, I am happy to see you occupying the position you do." The Colonel clasped the hand, and replied: "I am equally pleased, Ben, to see you enlisted on the side of law, order and good government; henceforth let us be friends." And these two brave men, who, a few years before had, in the heat of passion, engendered by bitter remarks made in a public speech, tried to shoot each other in the court-house at Irvine, Ky., buried there, by the surging waves of the Ohio, all their old differences of Whig and Democrat, henceforth to be brothers in arms against treason and rebellion. At 5 o'clock, p. m., all aboard, the planks were drawn in, and our fleet of five large river steamers rounded out into the swollen current of the river, the excellent band of the Third Minnesota playing "Hail Columbia." The men and officers of the fleet, being principally on the hurricane deck, cheered a long and loud adieu to Louisville. The swift current, aided by the revolving machinery, soon carried us from the view of the large crowd of spectators we left on the wharf.

The commissioned officers all took cabin passage, and we very soon discovered ourselves to be unwelcome passengers, especially on the "Nashville." Captain Barkley, part owner and captain of this boat, was evidently mad, as his boat had been pressed into the United States service for this trip.

He complained bitterly about the men being noisy, and objected to a few who were yet feeble occupying the spare berths in the rooms taken by their officers, who agreed to pay for them. While seated at the well-supplied supper table, Captain Banton and myself were speaking of Colonel Barnes and Captain Rice's mutual reconciliation, when our attention was drawn to the other end of the table by rather loud talk from one of the Eighth's officers and the engineer of the boat. Said the latter: "I cannot help sympathizing with the South; the Northern people have persistently for many years done all they could to cripple the interests of the slave-holding States, and their domestic institutions."

Captain Hickman—"There you are slightly mistaken, sir. When the Southern people, by the aid of a President favorable to slavery, tried to spread that curse of human rights over our fertile plains of the Northwest, the Northern emigrants there simply out-voted the advocates of negro slavery, and adopted Free-State constitutions."

To this the engineer only replied: "You've a d—d big job on hand, anyhow."

Lieutenant Park then said: "Well, sir, if your sympathies are so strong for the South, why don't you go and fight for your principles?"

To this the engineer replied: "I was not talking to you, sir, whom I take to be an impertinent puppy!"

Lieutenant Park, hastily pushing back his chair and raising to his feet, said: "I left home to shoot rebels and Jeff. Davis dogs, and will begin on you!"

Had it not been for an officer on each side of the Lieutenant seizing his pistols, no doubt we would have had a dead engineer on board. This same engineer hastily left the room, and we did not hear any more Southern gush during the trip, from him or any of the boat's crew.

On the morning of the 20th our fleet landed at Connelton, Ind., where a good supply of coal was taken on. During our stay a large crowd of citizens of the town, men, women, boys and dogs, collected on the bank, some, apparently, to show their loyalty, the girls their beauty, and the boys and dogs their combativeness. Two of the dogs yoked for a fight. Two boys, evidently the respective owners of the canine combatants, in endeavoring to command the peace, got mad, and with equal ferocity pitched into each other's wool. This animated scene caused loud cheers from the soldiers. Instantly all the bands of the fleet struck up lively music, and the machinery was soon in motion bearing us on down the Ohio. The officers of the Eighth on the "Nashville" overruled Barkley's objections to the men occupying spare berths, and had many of them take their meals at the table.

The night of the 20th being very dark, and the river out among the trees, with much drift in the center of the stream, our boat ran against a tree and threw every sleeper out of bed. Fortunately no serious injury was done to passengers or boat.

The evening of the 21st our fleet arrived at Smithland, situated at the mouth of the Cumberland River, and turned up that stream at 6 o'clock. We made slow progress against the strong current, and did not attempt to run after dark. A short run on the 22d brought us in sight of Fort Donaldson. We landed here, and some of us, understanding that the fleet would lay here several hours, struck out over the hill to view the late battlefield. We had only time to arrive on the rebels' old encampment, when the whistle of the boats gave us warning to return, and we did some tall double-quicking to secure further passage. Very soon we came in sight of the ruins of the once flourishing iron-works owned by the presidential aspirant, John Bell. Here about fifty negroes of both sexes, all ages and colors, had gathered themselves together on the river's bank. They made many demonstrations of joy, clapping their hands, swinging their hats and patting and dancing. The cheering of our men appeared to stimulate them to more vigorous bodily exertion. One old white-headed negro broke forth into singing:

> "O, praise and tanks! de Lord he come
> To set de people free;
> An' massa tink it day ob doom,
> An' we ob jubilee, &c."

The entire dusky crowd joining in the chorus, viz:

> "O, neber you fear if neber you hear
> De driver blow his horn!"

Our fleet lay by near Clarksville that night, and arrived at Nashville early on the 23d, meeting with no serious accident until early that morning. Private Frazier, wagoner of Company A, while attending to his mules, was by one of them pushed overboard and drowned before assistance could reach him. His body was not recovered, and probably became food for the fish. Thus, another good man was lost to the regiment and his country. Several hours were spent in disembarking and unloading forage, and at 2 o'clock, p. m., we left the boats. One boat officer at least was not sorry to part company with the "noisy Eighth," as he called us.

CHAPTER III.

As we marched through this beautiful Southern city on that pleasant, bright spring afternoon, solemn, silent sadness was depicted in the faces of the few white men that appeared on the sidewalks. Doors and windows of stores and dwelling houses were principally closed. Feminine curiosity caused a few ladies to peep from behind window shades. But hundreds of smiling "darkies" could be seen peeping around corners, and crowded into the unfrequented alleys, silently making demonstrations of joyous welcome to us.

We pitched our tents near the Murfreesboro Pike, two miles from Nashville, where our three regiments were joined by Colonel Duffield and the Ninth Michigan Infantry. Colonel Duffield immediately took command of the brigade. He proved to be a strict disciplinarian. During the six days we remained here we were not idle. There was vigorous drilling six hours of the day, winding up with dress parade, at which the Adjutants read to their respective regiments lengthy general orders of Major-General Buell, one among them being his " Roasting-ear Order," strictly forbidding soldiers entering private grounds or premises, on any plea whatever, without authority of their officers ; private property on no occasion to be taken for public use without due compensation, &c.

On the 28th, the Eighth received a new supply of clothing, dress coats and hats taking the place of soldier jackets and caps.

The 29th, the brigade marched six miles south on the Murfreesboro Pike. The rear guard, commanded by the author, had to wait at our old camp two hours for some wagons. During this time several aristocratic-looking slave-owners, followed by a train of little darkies, came to the vacant encampment, and began to gather up the many half-worn garments cast off by our boys. I said to one of the men: "I thought you Tennesseeans hated us Yankees so bitterly you would disdain to pick up our old clothes." He replied: "O, they will do for the niggers to wear." By my orders the guards soon had every rag heaped upon the fires, deeming it best not to furnish rebel spies suitable uniforms in which to enter our lines.

We pitched our tents that evening on an old rebel encampment. Here we made our first acquaintance with those army pests commonly called "greybacks." The rebels had, like ourselves, left cast-off garments, which appeared to be too lousy even for "nigger's" clothing.

Our mode of picketing at this time was to station a platoon out on all the roads leading into camp, and as John Morgan was reported to be scouting around Lebanon, Tenn., our pickets manifested great watchfulness.

The 30th, the Twenty-third Kentucky and the Ninth Michigan resumed the march southward, Colonel Barnes being ordered to remain here a few days with the Eighth Kentucky and furnish men and teams to cut and haul timber to rebuild the railroad bridge over Mill Creek, recently burned by the retreating rebels. The rank and file of the Eighth were much displeased to be left behind and do "drudgery," as some of the officers called it, while other regiments, no more experienced, were ordered on front, where probably fights and fame awaited them, and the Eighth were just "spoiling" for a battle. Big Bill Moore, Company H, remarked with much bitterness: "Now, Colonel Munday's regiment and them long-legged Michiganders will jest go ahead and scare out all the secesh, and won't leave a chicken or a pig in the hull country."

The next day eighty men, with teams and axes, were detailed for fatigue duty, and were early playing destruction with a fine grove of oaks. A much-excited Southern gentleman named Whitmore made his appearance, and in angry tones ordered the men to leave his premises. Lieutenant McDaniel pointed to Major Broadhus, who was seated on a log enjoying a quiet smoke, and told the indignant owner "That's the officer for you to consult."

Mr. Whitmore to Major Broadhus—"Sir, you appear to be doing me great injustice, taking my property without my consent."

Major B.—"Well, sir, what are you going to do about it?"

Mr. W.—"I don't know."

Major B.—"Well, neither do I know or care. Did

you try to persuade the rebels not to burn that bridge?"

Mr. W. (excitedly)—"No, sir; that was none of my business."

Major B.—"Well, neither is this any of your business."

The Major, pulling out his watch, said: "Now, you infernal rebel, I'll give you just three minutes to get out of sight, and if you don't, I will teach you by whose authority we are here, by trotting you all the way to Nashville about three inches in advance of a bayonet." He left instantly, but I have no doubt received in due time compensation for his fine timber.

Having finished our timber hauling, the 3d of April the regiment marched on the Murfreesboro Pike to Lavergne, there took the cross pike toward Woodbury, and camped on the West Fork of Stone River, near an ancient-looking little village called Old Jefferson. Resumed the march the 4th, and on arriving at the crossing of Stone River, on the Lebanon Pike, the rebels had burned the bridge, and during a hard rain we waded the stream. The stones were slippery and the current very swift, causing a great many self-immersions. Those who fell were about as comfortable as the others, all being thoroughly wet. We halted long enough to wring our stockings, arriving at Murfreesboro at 4 o'clock, p. m. We marched through town in column by companies, our musicians playing "Yankee Doodle." We saw but few of the inhabitants. They were evidently not pleased to see this second edition of Yankee troops.

Here we found Colonel Duffield, with the Ninth Michigan and the Twenty-third Kentucky, encamped near a large spring southeast of town. Two companies of the Seventh Pennsylvania Cavalry were also here. We remained here nearly one month. Our time was spent in drilling daily all those not required for camp guards and picket duty. The latter required 150 men and four officers from the Eighth, daily. Commissioned officers met two hours each morning in school, and one hour in practice of manual of arms, Lieutenant-Colonel May being a tight "school-master." Add to this the reviews, dress-parade, cooking, washing, &c., gave us but little time to idle. This constant duty and drill probably caused a few men to try feigning sick. At 7 o'clock, a. m., the bugle would sound that doleful call, and the sick assembled at the surgeon's tent, where they were excused from duty and prescribed for. Some of the boys concluded that others "were playing off" on Dr. Mills. One morning B. Ward, Company F, on being notified by his Orderly to "get ready for picket," replied: "Sergeant, I'll be blasted if anybody can't get excused that'l go to sick call, an' ef you'l let me, I'll prove it," and Ben's name was put down. At the bugle signal Ben wended his way slowly to the surgeon's tent, assuming a countenance of pain and misery calculated to deceive the "very elect." He awaited his turn. Surgeon Mills, knowing him to be a faithful soldier, asked the usual question: "What's the matter with you?" "O, 'Doc,' I am wrong every way in my innards." Ben soon had the satisfaction of seeing "ex" written opposite his name, and the steward gave him his pills, with directions. Ben had a fine day's sleep, and in the evening arose refreshed, and around the cook fire was engaged in a tight wrestle with one of his comrades. Doctor Mills just then passed, and was astonished to see such improvement in his late patient. With a volley of oaths he told Ben if he did not explain his evident deception he would have him tied up by the thumbs. Seeing an honest confession the safest way out of the dilemma, he gave the surgeon the cause of his assumed illness. This had the effect desired, and the surgeon became more careful in the future; also causing Ward, about a week later, to go on duty a very sick soldier, dismissing him from sick call with the command, "Sergeant, put that d—d hypocrite on duty; I don't believe he looks half as sick as he did when up here last." Ward never tried that dodge on Dr. Mills again.

Our manner of picketing all the roads with fifteen or twenty men and a cavalry vidette was kept up. On the 12th April a squad of the Eighth was posted on the Franklin Pike. Private Joe King, Company H, as sentinel, a little distance from the reserve, commanded a citizen to halt. As he was about to pass without paying any attention to the command, it was repeated. This time the man said, with an oath: "I'll not be halted by no d—d abolition

Yankee!" Seeing King raise his gun, the fellow broke to run, when King fired, killing him instantly. Colonels Duffield and Barnes both rode out to investigate the affair, and decided that the soldier only did his duty, commending him for his faithfulness. The citizens about town complained to Colonel Barnes bitterly of the shooting of a man whom they claimed was crazy. The Colonel told them if that was the case he was sorry, but if they did not want their fools killed they must take better care of them. People passing our pickets after that about Murfreesboro were careful to halt at the word.

During the two first weeks of our stay here many slaves came to our pickets, generally after dark. Colonel Duffield's orders were to send them in to the provost-marshal, their owners being allowed to come in and reclaim their slaves on condition of the masters taking an oath of loyalty to the United States Government, which some of them reluctantly did. But the general aversion of masters to comply with the condition very soon had Captain Rouns, provost-marshal, overstocked with this valuable species of Southern property. Colonel Duffield suggested to the officers of the Eighth the propriety of hiring our cooks from among these "contrabands," but we declined the idea of runaway negro cooks, as did also the Twenty-third Kentucky, we having not yet properly considered the slave a factor in this great war. The dusky sons of toil poured into the picket stations in such numbers we had to stop them from coming in, some of the officers threatening to punish them if they did not immediately return to their masters.

In looking back at this soft and easy policy of General Buell, we cannot wonder that the efforts of the first eighteen months to put down the rebellion were a failure. These hundreds of stout, able-bodied men, driven back into rebel corn and wheat-fields, that they might toil to produce subsistence for a large rebel army the next fall and winter, was anything but wisdom. But then we were trying to put down insurrection and let slavery alone, notwithstanding we knew the cruel taskmasters of these slaves to be the worst of enemies and rebels at heart.

On the 15th our brigade made quite a parade in the streets of Murfreesboro, and hoisted the stars and stripes on the court house. Nearly all the inhabitants of the town were silent spectators of what they evidently thought to be an insult to their Southern pride. Lieutenant Colonel Parkhurst, of the Ninth Michigan, made an appropriate and sensible speech to the citizens, in which he admonished them to return to their loyalty, "And," said he, "we will then kill the fatted calf." But as long as we remained there we heard of no fat calf being sacrificed in welcome to returning rebels, though we have good reason to believe, had a careful search been made in Stone River, quite a number of pig skins could have been found, securely attached to stones to insure their remaining at the bottom. Nor did we hear of any citizen ever being invited to feast on the savory pork those same skins once enveloped. Colonel Duffield had profound respect for Buell's orders regarding foraging, holding the officer immediately in command responsible for any violation of said orders. The author remembers having to pay three dollars for a sixty-pound shoat some of my picket guard had killed while I was absent visiting another post under my command. In this instance the old rebel complaining to Colonel Duffield, lyingly alleged the pig to belong to one of his old negro men. On hunting up this much-injured darkey, with the full intention of healing his lacerated feelings, and carrying out "general orders," the old fellow said : "Fo' de good Lord, Mars Cap'n, 'twant no mo' my pig dan dis farm is; ole mars' pig, sho'." On confronting "ole mars" with his bogus owner of the defunct swine, with much fear and trembling the old darkey lyingly confessed the pig to have been his. I gave the poor old scared nig the money, at the same time telling Miller if he took the money away from the negro we would surely call on him again, and that to his sorrow. Colonel Duffield was satisfied with the manner of my settlement for pork, but no more complaint was heard from Miller of lost pork, though some of the Eighth boys said when we left there that Miller was not overstocked with hogs.'

On the evening of the 23d April a dress-parade order was read detailing Lieutenant C. Park assistant brigade quartermaster. That night we were aroused from sleep by loud cheering and beating of drums in the Ninth's camp. Very soon Colonel Barnes had the Eighth assembled before his tent. He mounted a cracker box and said: "Brother officers and soldiers, we have just received orders to march to-morrow morning for Pittsburg Landing; boys, are you ready to go?" The response was loud and long cheering. At repeated calls Major Broadhus stepped on the box and said: "Boys, I am no speaker, but if we go to Pittsburg, I want it understood I'll try to make one in the fight." Orders were given to prepare three days' rations and have arms cleaned up. The regiment spent the balance of the night in cooking, washing and letter-writing.

At 9 o'clock the 24th we were ready formed, waiting the order to march, when an order was received countermanding the order of the previous night, John Morgan, with quite a force of rebel cavalry, having made a raid on Wartrace, and still being in the cedars toward Lebanon, being the cause of our detention here.

The 26th, Companies C, E, D and I, of the Eighth, under command of Major Broadhus, were ordered on the train to Shelbyville, thirty miles further south, to relieve some troops there. Many flying rumors of Morgan's near approach caused us to be on the *qui vive*.

The 28th, Colonel Wolford and Colonel Clay Smith, with two regiments of Kentucky cavalry, succeeded in overtaking Morgan, at Lebanon, Tenn., completely routing the rebels and driving them into

Kentucky. We were rejoiced at the news of the capture of New Orleans.

Paymaster Hunes paid off the regiment the 29th—two months' pay.

The 3d day of May, Colonel Barnes, with the balance of the regiment able for duty, except Captain Thomas and Company K, double-quicked to the depot, boarded a train of platform cars, and were soon landed at Wartrace. Company K, with the baggage wagons, arrived in a few days after. The four companies under Major Broadhus, a few days after, rejoined the regiment. Company C, Captain Wilson commanding, was detached to guard the railroad bridge over Duck River, about one mile south of Wartrace, and Company H, Captain Winbourn commanding, to the bridge over Carter's Creek, one and a half miles north of the latter place. The eight companies there worked with their usual vigor for more than a week, felling trees and forming abattis, and otherwise fortifying against cavalry. For the first two weeks of our stay here some rebel cavalry, under Colonel Starnes, hanging around Beech Grove, between us and McMinnville, kept our pickets on the *qui vive*, almost nightly expecting an attack.

Colonel Runkle, with a part of the Fourth Kentucky Cavalry, encamped also at Wartrace, succeeded in picking up a few rebel prisoners. Scouting parties from the Eighth also occasionally brought in a few prisoners, principally men who had been temporarily connected with or given material aid to the rebel cause. Some of them took the oath of loyalty, and were released. Others, who were evidently active enemies, and somewhat saucy, Colonel Barnes put to grubbing out stumps from the Eighth's drill grounds.

Colored men from the surrounding country, in their well-meant zeal to be of service to us, often came at night to our camp, with alarming reports that a body of rebel cavalry were about to attack us. These reports generally proved to be unfounded, though on one occasion, timely warning by a colored man, who came to Captain Winbourn, at Carter's Creek, and reported that Colonel Dibrell's cavalry were only five miles from us, proved true, and probably saved Company H from attack, as reinforcement of that company by the cavalry at Wartrace, and rebel citizens living near us gave Dibrell this intelligence, and the intended attack was not made. The company lay on their arms behind the railroad embankment all that night, however, and rather anxious to be attacked, and our cavalry reinforcement returned to camp also disappointed.

This Company H, to which the author belonged, kept about one-half on guard at a time during the night, as long as we remained here, with the other half dressed, with accoutrements buckled on, ready for instant action. But the oft-threatened attack never came while we remained.

At dusk on the evening of the 6th May, Colonel Barnes sent a squad of the Fourth Cavalry to our company camp, with an order for Lieutenant Wright and a squad of the company to go with the cavalry and assist in capturing a rebel surgeon who had remained in the neighborhood since the little fight here two weeks before. The cavalry had twice ran him from his home into a heavy wood near and failed to effect his capture. I selected Sergeant Winbourn, and privates Dennis, P. Elliot, H. Morris and two others. We proceeded, in company with the cavalry. On the way we met a negro man. I stopped him and inquired if he knew where Dr. Nusen lived. "Yes, sah; he's ole mars' son-en-law, an' he's de berry debbel on niggers." Said I, "Do you know if he's at home or not?" "Yes, mars, I speck he's dah." We took the negro along for a guide. The cavalry halted half a mile from the doctor's house, which was situated near a new pike road, while the infantry, accompanied by the guide, took a circuitous course through a dense forest, coming up in the rear of the premises. After we were properly deployed behind the garden fence, the preconcerted signal was given to the cavalry, which charged down the rough pike, making a terrible clatter. At the same time we rushed up in the back yard, where a savage-looking dog made a spring at one of the boys, who succeeded in thrusting his bright steel bayonet through the savage beast, and left him howling piteously. As we closed up around the house, I met the object of our search at the back door, dressed in his night clothes, with an overcoat and a quilt on his arm. He was about to jump out into the darkness, when he caught sight of my pistol and heard my command to surrender about the same time. He said: "I suppose I shall have to, as you have the drop on me." Three of us entered the house with the prisoner, where he was allowed to dress. This sudden and somewhat noisy proceeding, with continued deafening howls of the dog, had frightened the two women and other gentleman very much. After assuring them no one should be hurt, I asked for all the firearms about the place. They at first denied having any except the pistol taken from the doctor. But when informed that a search would be made, Mrs. N. said she had a little "lady's pistol," which proved to be a good-sized five-shooter, ready capped and loaded. I informed her that, if that was the kind of jewelry that was fashionable with the Southern ladies, we were decidedly opposed to it, and took the pistols, and placed them and the doctor in charge of the cavalry, who reported to Colonel Barnes. As we left the premises we heard our black guide trying to suppress his laughter, being hid near the road.

About the 12th May, the small pox broke out among the soldiers of the regiment, but the prompt and judicious management of Surgeon Mills prevented it from spreading, and confined it to the five first cases.

After our fortifications were completed the regiment's duty consisted principally of guard duty and drill. Lieutenant Colonel May generally conducted the battalion drills of the eight companies at headquarters. At the same time Companies C and H, stationed at the bridges, improved much in company drill. But as the author only made a few short visits to headquarters during the six weeks we remained at Wartrace, many interesting events of personal adventure by that part of the command cannot be given, and I shall only give a few relating to Company H.

Our tents were pitched in the creek bottom, where the land had many years before been cleared of timber and well set in grass. The cows of the entire neighborhood ran at large, and about one-half of them wore bells. At night the noise of the bells on cattle trying to browse on our drill ground annoyed us so much that we notified the citizens to keep them away, or we might be forced to shoot them. Our greatest danger was attack from cavalry, and quietude enables a sentinel to hear the trampling horses a great distance.

After we suppressed the cows, it seemed that as soon as night spread its shades over earth every worthless cur within five miles (and there were many) tried to make night hideous with barking and howling. Many of these half-starved whelps came nightly to our camp on the hunt for waste grub. Anxious as were the boys to shoot them, it could not be done without causing unnecessary alarm in the regiment, only one and a half miles distant ; therefore, during the day, many little piles of stones were placed convenient for use after dark. In two weeks it was perfectly safe for a stranger to approach residences in that vicinity, as every dog that survived was utterly unable for duty as a watch dog.

The 29th May, the Union citizens in the neighborhood held what was intended to be a Union meeting. The principal part of the Eighth Kentucky attended and enjoyed the hospitality of the citizens. Many inhabitants were also there of well-known rebel sentiments. Colonel Barnes made the principal speech, pointing out to his audience the advantages to the South, especially Tennessee, to remain in the Union, and the certainty of ultimate defeat of the rebels, and consequent disgrace, and the financial ruin the South would suffer, winding up, in his usual earnest manner, with a warning to the disloyal to "flee from the wrath to come." That night many of the officers and men of the Eighth wound up the meeting with a ball at the hotel, kept by Haley, alias "Pig-tracks." I was informed by those present that many of the fair damsels of the country attended, and took much pleasure in whirling their high-priced calico in graceful cotillions with the hateful Yankees until daylight.

Probably every regiment and company in the service had their slovenly, awkward, but good-natured, lazy member. Company H certainly had one in Aldrich, whom the boys nick-named "Dobin Spikes." If any member of the company was later getting out at roll-call than "Dobin," he was invariably marked "absent." On inspection he was sure to have the rustiest gun, and his knapsack contained the dirtiest clothing. The captain had been mildly reprimanding "Dobin" for his untidy appearance, but he seemed not to heed the reproof. One Sunday morning, at Carter's Creek, Captain W. was absent, and Lieutenant Cox inspected the company. "Dobin," as usual, had on a dirty shirt, face and neck ditto, and hair longer than usual. Lieutenant Cox gave him a severe scolding, and cautioned him never to appear at inspection again in that condition. The next Sunday morning, Lieutenant Cox being sick, the duty of inspecting the company devolved on the author. "Dobin's" shirt-collar and neck had no appearance of recent contact with soap and water. His tangled flaxen locks had gained one more week's growth, his gun and accoutrements were in keeping with his neglected person. I passed him by without a single reproof or remark. After dismissing the company, I ordered the sergeant to arrest "Dobin," and bring him to the captain's tent. Sergeant Morris, with a sharp pair of scissors, soon parted "Dobin" and his cherished, but neglected, golden locks. S. Wood and two other boys were then ordered to take "Dobin" to the creek and wash his neck for him. Feeling certain they would do up a good job, I laid down in my tent. Soon after, hearing much loud laughter at the creek bank, interspersed with terrible oaths from "Dobin's" well-known voice, I walked down. In the middle of the stream stood the now furious "Dobin," firmly held by two stout men. Wood, with a bar of soap in one hand and two corncobs in the other, was rubbing the swearing, struggling victim's neck, which, with rubbing and his anger, had, chamelion-like, assumed a clean, reddish appearance. I told the men to let Mr. Aldrich finish his morning ablution unassisted. After that no more orders had to be given about hair-trimming, and "Dobin" thereafter paid considerable attention to his Sunday toilet.

The regiment was again paid the 7th of June, by Major Davies, up to the 1st of May. On the 9th, a large number of the Eighth were detailed to cut timbers for the rebuilding of the railroad bridge over Duck River, and on the evening of the 10th the camp was in unusual commotion, with orders to cook two days' rations, and be ready to march early the next morning. At sunrise, the 11th, Captain Winbourn, with Company H, and Captain Wilson and Company C, joined the regiment, leaving the tents and the principal part of the garrison equipage in charge of some convalescents. At 9 o'clock, being joined by the Twenty-first Kentucky, a part of the Fourth Kentucky Cavalry, and a few pieces of artillery, marched toward McMinnville, passed through Fairfield, and camped for the night in the hills at the head of McBride's Creek, in Coffee County. The 12th we camped within six miles of McMinnville, on Collins River, having passed through poor, brushy country. The inhabitants appeared to be still poorer, and evidently much alarmed at the sight of so many real live Yankees. Early the 13th, we waded Collins River, which was waist deep and very swift. A good number of us got our greenbacks wet. We entered McMinnville, the county seat of Warren County, about 8 o'clock a. m., and bivouacked in the suburbs, near a large cotton factory, working about one hundred women, making cloth for the Confederates. But as we were now carrying on the war under General Buell's policy, i. e. respecting private property—though we had every reason to believe it would be used to feed or clothe the enemy—the spindles and looms kept on.

We were here joined by General Dumont, with three or four thousand troops from Murfreesboro, and early the 14th the whole force passed through town and struck out for the Sequatche Valley, over the Cumberland Mountains. We had seven miles of good road to the Barren fork of Collins River. Here the troops were allowed to undress before wading the river. This mode of ferrying was rather enjoyed by the troops than otherwise. But to the great displeasure of our regiment, we were detailed as train guard, and the whole regiment assisted the drivers in getting up the mountain, which, here at Hill's Creek Gap, is two miles from the base to the summit, in many places so steep our men were compelled to push the entire weight of the loaded wagons and artillery, it being all the mules and horses could do to carry up their own weight, the teamsters and men swearing profanely enough to have disgusted the "Army of Flanders." Near sunset we reached the top of the mountain, weary and foot sore; every canteen in the regiment empty, with twelve miles of mountain ridge road before us, and not a spring, stream or a human habitation near our road; at the same time our lank haversacks admonishing us to diet light. The lumbering wagons and profane teamsters rolled ahead while we tramped on nearly famishing with thirst. About one o'clock a. m. the 15th, we came up with our main force, bivouacked at a large mountain spring of good water. We ate the last of our rations and for two hours enjoyed refreshing sleep, but before sun-rise the whole force were drummed and bugled up, and off again on sore feet and empty stomachs. Near noon, as we were marching on at the head of the column, bright visions of the fat hens and smoking pones of corn bread just a few miles ahead in the promised land of Sequatche Valley, where we were promised plenty, if not peace. Alas, "there is many a slip between the cup and the lip." General Dumont met a courier with a dispatch from General Mitchell to return with his troops to their former camps. At the command "counter-march by file right, march," as the head of our column filed around on the back track, some of our boys gave vent to their disgusted feelings. One member of Company D yelled out, " Now, by G—d, I feel like killing something." That afternoon we did kill a few poor cows the Fourth Kentucky Cavalry brought in out of the brush. Late that evening we arrived at the spring we left in the morning. The line officers of the Eighth remonstrated against the order to proceed on to Collins River. We informed Colonel Barnes that our men went no further until we had opportunity of cooking and eating some of our scrub beef, which we did there and then, broiling it on the coals, and, without salt or bread, this tough, stringy, burnt meat was eaten, being washed down with coffee, which our boys were fortunate in having. In spite of Dumont's orders, our regiment slept here until 2 o'clock next morning. Our band awoke us, and by a bright, full moon we made good time to Collins River, keeping our men well in ranks. We passed whole companies of stragglers from other regiments, whose officers had tried to force their men to comply with Dumont's order. On arriving at the river at noon we met wagons with rations of hard bread and good side bacon, and a couple of barrels of whisky for the 6,000 troops. Men who one hour before had been cursing "old Dumont," were now praising him as the best of generals. We arrived at McMinnville near night, and the general compelled citizens to furnish his troops bread. Some of them certainly knew how to make the staff of life palatable.

The following day the Eighth and Twenty-first Kentucky marched twenty miles on our road toward Wartrace. While at halt that evening a member of Company K accidentally discharged his gun, severely wounding Jo. Derbin, Company D, in the foot. The night of the 18th we bivouacked near Beach Grove, and arrived at noon, the 19th, at our respective encampments at and near Wartrace, and resumed our regular guard duty and daily drilling. That evening Company H had two of its company mules killed by a locomotive, upsetting the train and killing the engineer.

CHAPTER IV.

The 23d June, Adjutant John Clark and Captain Winbourn obtained leave of absence and started to Kentucky.

The afternoon of the 4th day of July our company drill suddenly stopped by the reception of an order from Colonel Barnes for Company H to get aboard the train that bore us the order and rejoin the regiment forthwith. Leaving our tents and garrison equipage in charge of a sergeant and ten men, we arrived at Wartrace at sun set, where all the regiment except details from each company to guard the tents, &c., boarded our train of platform cars, and, as the whistle sounded and the iron wheels began moving South, the Eighth gave three cheers, and bid Wartrace and old "Pig-tracks" farewell; halted two hours at Tullahoma, and as we were settling down to a pleasant nap of sleep, orders were given to "fall in," "fall in;" "all aboard for Alisona!" The moon shone brightly. A short run of nine miles brought us to Elk River bridge, or where the bridge had been destroyed by the rebels. Near midnight the Eighth left the train, crossed the stream, many getting wet by slipping off the treacherous old dam that once turned the water on to the busy wheels of a flourishing cotton factory, the charred ruins of which made us feel sad. Viewed by the light of a waning moon, the desolation was doubly solemn. We took possession of the score or more of vacated houses that constituted the town where the toiling employes had dwelt, and were soon oblivious to things past and present.

Early the 5th, a large detail from the Eighth were put to cutting timber to rebuild the railroad bridge. Several days were spent in assisting the government employes. The 7th July the Eighth made a general cleaning of arms, and many washed their clothes. A few rebel citizens came into camp, and others, who had been in the confederate service, were brought in by the Seventh Pennsylvania Cavalry. Some of them appeared more eager to trade with "you ens" than they were to take the oath of loyalty. One tow-headed fellow swore, " I haint hed a chaw uv terbaccer nor a grain uv salt in my house fur four months."

Our accommodating sutler, R. Keneday, followed us up the 8th with a fresh supply of army goods, but scarcely had time to unload before we were ordered back to Tullahoma, and the greater part of that night our cooks were busy boiling and frying the two days' rations.

Early the 9th, one of those hot, sultry, spiritless mornings, our men were ordered to pile their knapsacks by the railroad track in charge of the orderlies of each company, and thus, freed from some of the weight, the regiment marched northward. The low, distant thunder and ominous, dark clouds came nearer. At 9 o'clock, a. m., the rain began to pour down on us in torrents. Arriving at Tullahoma depot, the regiment stacked arms, and the men sought shelter until the train and the sergeants, with the knapsacks, arrived. The men had neglected marking their property, so as to readily recognize it from that of their comrades, which resulted in much confusion, swearing and overhauling of knapsacks. Meantime Colonel Barnes added to the confusion by hurrying and swearing for the regiment to form. Our camp and garrison equipage having met us here, we pitched our tents half a mile west of town. As the rain continued nearly all night, almost every member of the regiment got thoroughly wet in erecting tents. The next day was spent in sunning and drying bedding and clothing. To avoid another knapsack squabble, several of the Eighth officers procured paint and lettered the knapsacks.

Here the Thirty-fifth Indiana, the Irish regiment, was added to the Eighth and Twenty-first Kentucky, forming the Twenty-third Brigade, Colonel Barnes temporarily in command. The 11th, the First Kentucky Battery and Fifth Kentucky Cavalry, Colonel Haggard, arrived from Wartrace. The 12th, Companies D and I, of the Eighth, were sent as guard to Elk River, as the enemy's cavalry were menacing several points north and south of us.

Early Sunday morning, the 13th, while the Eighth were generally engaged in devouring salt pork and crackers, cannonading could be heard north of us. Late that evening we learned that Forrest, with a force of cavalry, had, after a brief fight with Colonel Lester, Third Minnesota and Ninth Michigan, taken Murfreesboro and burned the depot, taking a good many of the Ninth prisoners, and among them Lieutenant Park, Sergeant Elkin and private Johnson, of our regiment. The latter part of the report proved untrue. Lieutenant Park, by the assistance of the family with whom he was boarding, eluded the rebels by secreting himself in the cellar. The other two played off citizens on the rebels, who only held the town a few hours.

About this time Bragg's and Kirby Smith's troops in and below Chattanooga began to feel their way northward, which caused a part of Buell's army, under General Smith, to concentrate about 12,000 infantry and cavalry here to resist an expected attack from rebel cavalry. About 3,000 of General Wood's command arrived at Elk River, and our two companies rejoined us. The morning of the 15th, we moved into town, and, with other troops, began fortifying the place, as later reports confirmed the rumor of a large rebel force from Chattanooga making their way toward this place. A large force felled trees while others threw up a line of earthworks encircling the town. At the same time a large number of wagons were sent out over the country under strong guard, to collect a supply of flour and other provisions. A string of pickets were placed around the place, and artillery placed in good position. All this began to look like war in earnest. To husband our half rations of beef and flour, Companies C and H of the Eighth, while on picket the 16th, took the precaution to lay in a good supply of pork and potatoes, the latter, as S. Wood, remarked, he "jest found growing wild up yonder in a patch of weeds," and Burgess, Company H, said "the rebel hog hadn't the countersign." After all this preparation for a siege, our men appeared somewhat disappointed, the evening of the 8th, to learn that the enemy had fallen back, and we were ordered to march back to Murfreesboro, via Shelbyville. Accordingly, the 19th, we loaded our train, and, with the other three regiments of our brigade, marched northwest, over poor country, meeting part of General Wood's division. Encamped early, within ten miles of Shelbyville. The 20th, after passing over a very rough road, we arrived at that town at noon, where we cooked and ate dinner. That evening we made a short march of eight miles, and bivouacked on the Murfreesboro Pike, in a fine section of country, large, well cultivated fields of splendid crops of corn and cotton, with occasional stacks of wheat. The slaves were yet generally at home. The face of the country showed no ravages of war, thanks to Buell's orders and the mild manner of the administration in dealing with these aristocratic slave-owners, who were principally in the field fighting to destroy the government, while their slaves were raising bountiful supplies to feed the rebel army the coming winter. It mattered not how much our tired, hungry soldiers wished a mess of green corn as a change from our hard-tack, not an ear of corn, or peach, or apple could be had without violating general orders. Many staff and line officers had become disgusted with enforcing these strict orders and this "conciliatory policy" of putting down the rebellion, and did not see a few green cobs lying about camp fires before the boys had managed to bury or secrete them.

The 21st July, we arrived at Murfreesboro, where we made our first acquaintance with Colonel Stanley Matthews and the Fifty-first Ohio, that regiment here being added to our brigade, formed the Third Brigade of the Third Division of the Twenty-first Army Corps. Colonel Matthews being sick, Colonel Barnes continued in command. General Nelson, commanding the division, on the morning of the 22d, went with all the division except the Third Brigade on a scout toward Manchester, while our four regiments marched back through town, crossed the river near the charred remains of the depot, and laid off a line of rifle pits. A heavy detail from each regiment was put to digging. Colonel Barnes also sent out guards under commissioned officers in every direction, with orders to conscript every able-bodied negro man they could find and bring them in to assist in fortifying. By 10 o'clock a. m., we had about two hundred stout, well-pleased darkies heaving up the earth. The officers and men that had collected this dusky force related some amusing incidents of the talk and action of some of those "masters" who remonstrated against having their "niggers" do work for the Yankees. Capt. Minter and a squad of the 8th entered the premises of a rich planter, whom with his two sons were in the rebel army, an old negro man named Jim, conducting affairs on the farm for his mistress. Soon the guards had "Boss" Jim and seven or eight other negro men assembled in the road near the fine house. The mistress appeared on the portico, and totally ignoring the presence of the captain and his men, she addressed "Jim," saying, "I would like to know what you mean by leaving your work and bringing in the other hands?" Jim, pulling off his hat, replied, "Missus, we's gwine to town wid dese jemmen to work." Lady—"Now you take the hands right back to that field this minute or you'll have to account for it, certain." "Missus, I can't, I'se bound to 'bey dese sojers. Dese are malicious orders, missus, and I'se bound to 'spect dem." The captain with his conscript force moved off, leaving the indignant "missus" in the porch heaping abuse on the whole Yankee army. The darkies worked zealously — they evidently thought themselves honored by such service and enjoyed their ration of "hard tack" and coffee very much. By sunset the long line of earthworks were completed. Col. Barnes received a dispatch from General Nelson, stating if we were not attacked before, to march with the 3d Brigade precisely at 2 o'clock next morning out on Lebanon pike, to attack a force of rebel cavalry, then at the river six miles from us. One day's rations were cooked, a few hours for sleep, then all the command able for duty formed column without a loud word or any noise that could possibly be avoided. The measured tramp, tramp of our feet through the silent streets of Murfreesboro by the dim starlight, awoke many of the slumbering citizens. Heads were thrust out of windows, but no questions asked. We silently but speedily moved on arriving at the ford of Stone River at the first glimmer of dawn, hoping and expecting to be able to dash on to the enemy and try our hand at mortal combat, but the cautious Johnnies had mounted their "critters" and left one hour before. Some of our men petulantly remarked, "That's jest our luck." After wading the river, we halted one hour for breakfast.

Colonel Barnes then ordered us forward on the Lebanon Pike, and to march as fast as we could, and keep the men well in the ranks. The day was oppressively hot and water scarce. At noon we were within ten miles of Lebanon, and halted for a little rest before proceeding to where we were assured we would have all the fighting we wanted. Just then a courier from Nelson handed Colonel Barnes an order for us to countermarch to Murfreesboro as quick as possible. Nearly every man had sore feet, but at the word of command, knapsacks were slung, arms taken, and, ho! for Murfreesboro again. When within two miles of Stone River, our advance guard fell back and reported a large force of rebel infantry at the ford. Colonel Barnes instantly had skirmishers put forward. The brigade trampled down a good-sized field of corn in hastily forming line of battle. We were all ready, and just then in the humor to fight anything, human or devil. A courier came dashing up and informed our colonel that the supposed enemy was General Nelson and the balance of the division. Many of the Eighth swore they had rather it had been the enemy, for, said they, "Here we've been out soldiering nearly twelve months, and but few of us have seen an armed rebel." The brigade bivouacked at the forks of the Lebanon and Woodbury Pikes. Our men did very little cooking or eating. We were too tired for anything except sleep, which we enjoyed with no more preparation of beds than a drove of stock.

We were bugled up early the 24th, and had hastily marched to within three miles of Murfreesboro, when we were again met by one of General Nelson's orders to countermarch. At this unexpected command, Chandler Branson, Company D, yelled out, "Now, by the blood of Balaam, ef this don't beat all." Some member of Company A, Eighth Kentucky, retorted, "I bet, by G—d, old Nelson or somebody's drunk." Our brigade returned to the cross roads before alluded to, and were reinforced by a squadron of the Fifth Kentucky Cavalry. We remained here two days, keeping out a strong chain of pickets to prevent any force of the enemy passing toward Nashville. Several bodies of rebel cavalry were then scouting around through the cedars that skirt the mountains in Middle Tennessee.

The 25th, General Nelson reviewed the Third Brigade, after which he put us through a "knapsack" drill, in brigade and battalion movements, cursing the Eighth for some blunders, but praising us for the correct performance of other movements. Whatever may have been his opinion of the Eighth, we certainly did not form a favorable one of this swearing, blustering old tar. A month's acquaintance did not increase our respect or love for him, though we all became thoroughly convinced of two prominent traits of Nelson's character: First, brave in the face of the foe; second, overbearing to all subordinates.

The 26th, a foraging party, commanded by Major Broadhus, of the Eighth Kentucky, and composed of Companies H and C, of the Eighth, and two companies of the Twenty-first, with twenty wagons, proceeded through the cedars, up Stone River, eight miles to a mill owned by a violent rebel named Tilford, where the soldiers, assisted by a lot of slaves, loaded the wagons with corn. No white man or woman could be seen. Major Broadhus said to a patriarchal darkey:

"Old man, where are the white people of this place?"

"Missus an de chillen is to her mudder's, an I speck mars is wid dem oder kind ob sojers."

Major Broadhus—"Did he leave you to manage affairs here?"

"Yes, sah; doh he tole me dis way to do, say he: 'Jake, you keep de mill a grinden de corn, an if you see de Yankees comin wid wagons, you jes set fire to de cribs and burn up de corn.'"

Major B.—"You don't seem to obey your master. When you saw us, why didn't you burn it?"

"Yah, yah, mars, I knowed den it do nobody any good, nor him, neder."

The wagons returned to the command without accident, and while the Eighth were at supper, the bugle sounded the officers' call. Soon we were collected around our chief. Colonel Barnes said: "Officers, I want you to get your men ready to march to Murfreesboro, and that d—d quick, for the General expects to be attacked by 8,000 rebels before daylight." As we had no baggage, we were soon wading the river, being the fourth time within four days. We arrived at Murfreesboro about midnight, and lay on our arms in line of battle near town, on the Woodbury Pike. Our men began to think this very hard soldiering, but it was only the beginning of our hardships. The line of battle was maintained until after sunrise the 27th, but the 8,000 enemy did not appear.

We received orders from General Nelson to prepare for a march in light order, specifying that the men would turn over their knapsacks to the quartermaster, the officers to be allowed to carry only one trunk or chest to three officers, and two tent-flies to a company of officers. Accordingly, all this extra baggage was marked and stored at Murfreesboro. This being completed by noon, General Nelson ordered every regiment out to drill two hours— the first and last time we ever drilled on Sunday.

We remained here without any further alarms until the morning of the first of August. The whole division, 8,000 strong, marched out on the McMinnville road, all with canteens full, as Nelson never allowed a man to leave ranks. The sun shone down on the stone road with powerful heat. We called a halt at noon for two hours, at a creek, then kept our men well in ranks, and arrived at Woodbury, the county town of Cannon County, at dark, having marched twenty-eight miles. As we had but little cooking to do, those not on guard were soon sleeping the sleep of the weary, if not that of the just.

The 2d, the division was aroused by the bugles and drums long before daylight, our hasty breakfast over, and the column in motion before the sun had showed his burning face.

We had correct information that General Forrest, with a brigade of rebel cavalry, was at McMinnville, and our men generally were anxious to bring the enemy at bay, and try our hand in a battle. General Nelson's threat to catch Forrest or kill the last man in the division, increased our desires to come up with the foe at as early a date as possible, for many of the command believed our general to mean what he said; and before that month had passed nearly all of the Eighth began to think him to be in dead earnest.

About 3 o'clock p. m. our advance came on the rebel pickets within a few miles of McMinnville. As they caught sight of our advance cavalry, they fired a few shots and fled toward town. We hastened on, arriving there near night, but no armed enemy could be seen. We stacked arms on the skirts of town and were anxiously expecting a distribution of rations. We had began to get used to disappointments and unpleasant surprises. One was here ready for Companies C, D, E and H, of the Eighth—we were ordered out on picket without the desired and much-needed grub. Several hours were spent is establishing the picket line so as to connect with the regular chain around town.

A few of the officers, including the author, called at some of the suburban residences and succeeded in arousing the not overly pleased inmates and succeeded in procuring some provisions, paying a good round price; thus our men, on a divide, secured sufficient to abate their gnawing hunger.

The whole division was kept in suspense all day the 3d, all being held in readiness to "march at a moment's warning." We slept there in line on our arms, and at daylight, the 4th, the whole command marched in quick time toward Sparta, Tenn. Five companies, B, H, G, K and I, of the 8th Kentucky, were detailed as rear guard, a duty all soldiers dislike, having to march behind the wagon train and artillery. We had not proceeded but a few miles, when, at the ford of Collins river, in a narrow piece of road, one wagon upset, and delayed the whole train for over two hours. This put us a long distance behind our column. Our Quartermasters and wagon-masters having more dread of old Nelson than they had of the enemy, made everything double quick for about ten miles, before the rear was properly closed up. We guards, of course, were compelled to regulate our march to keep pace with the hurrying train. Near night the artillery and wagons began to cross Cany Fork of the Cumberland River. The troops had crossed and climbed the mountain on the south side. Some of the teamsters while at a halt had found a house where they procured a supply of Tennessee brandy, and had followed the example of our division general, and imbibed too freely of the exhilarating fluid. On arriving at the stream, these boozy commanders of mules had, without orders, unhitched their teams. A few of the wagon-masters, no less sober, were powerless to command their trains. At this unpleasant state of affairs, the rain began to pour down in the manner it usually does in this latitude. All teamsters and their superiors that were yet sober, appeared to be like our guards, not in an enviable temper, and had Gen. Nelson been present, and refrained from swearing long enough to have heard the amount of profanity indulged in at that ford, he certainly would have been disgusted with this foolish habit. In the meantime we arrived upon the scene, and Col. Barnes, who could, on slight provocation, swear equal to an army teamster, rode around with a drawn weapon among the boozy teamsters and made them hitch up, and once more put the train in motion.

The principal part of our five companies worked hard all night by reliefs pushing wagons and artillery up the mountain. Every one of us, from colonel down, had our clothing thoroughly wet. In order to get a few hours' sleep without laying down in mud and water, I lashed my weary body to a tree trunk, using one of the men's gun straps and my own sword belt. While thus suspended, I slept quite sound.

About sun rise the next morning the last wagon topped the mountain. Without taking time to eat breakfast, we struck out in quick time to overtake the division, and soon came up with the column. After forced march of five miles, the head of the division met a scout. General Nelson had a brief interview with him, then commanded the column to " counter march, quick time, march!" This was to us discouraging, to say the least. But Nelson had been informed by Buell that we were about to meet the principal part of General Bragg's army, and that discretion was in this case, probably, the best. But our men said, " Here, we've lost sleep, waded rivers and ran around in the cedars until our shoes are worn out trying to meet the enemy, and now, when we are about to find the armed rebels, to retreat is worse than to fight and get whipped."

At the crossing of the river, the Eighth refused to go farther until we had time to get some rations out of the trains and get on the outside of that grub, which we did, regardless of friends in front or foes behind. Satisfying our hunger, we resumed the march and arrived at McMinnville a little before midnight.

On this nineteen miles of rough road this division of as good men as the United States had in the field left more stragglers than they probably ever did afterward. They all came up during the next day.

We pitched our tent flies in a large apple orchard northeast of town. The heavy crop of green fruit of that orchard totally disappeared within twenty-four hours—fried, with plenty of sugar added, making a good dish to a hungry soldier.

On the evening of the 6th, at dress parade, several of Nelson's troublesome orders were read; one of them requiring every regiment in the division to have battalion drill for two hours before breakfast; that at 7 o'clock, compelled us to be up and in line at 5, and from that until supper no time was lost from drill and other duties, except two hours for dinner. This lively exercise to men whose feet were yet very sore, was anything but pleasant recreation.

On the 9th of August, the Eighth escaped the ordeal of a knapsack drill, by an order sending us one mile out on the Smithville road as pickets. We remained there in the brush until the morning of the 11th, encountering no worse enemy than innumerable little insects called "seed ticks." The enemy was reported to have a large force at Smithville, twenty miles distant from us, and our boys were given strict orders. At a late hour on the night of the 10th, General Nelson and staff passed outside our pickets and returned by the Smithville route. Leaving the main road they came tearing along the by-road, evidently to try the mettle of our pickets. When within hailing distance, John W. Barnett, Company H, commanded "halt." Nelson and escort appeared not to hear, and John, in a loud voice, repeated, "Halt, there! or by Jupiter, I'll put a hole through one of you," at the same time all six of the men's pieces gave that ominous click that generally causes even a brave man to halt, and the General did, at the same time he said, "Who in the hell are you, to presume to halt a general officer and staff?" The reply was, "One of you dismount, advance and give the countersign, or we'll show you who we are, and that devilish quick." An aid obeyed this last summons, and Corporal Harris hallowed out, "The General and escort can pass in."

The moon shone brightly, and the boys knew Nelson before he advanced. His only remark as he passed in was, "By G—d; these Kentucks won't do to fool with."

As the force reported at Smithville did not come to attack us, on the morning of the 11th our brigade now under command of Col. Matthews, received orders to go in search of the Johnnies. The dirt road was rough from the dried mud of recent rains, and the weather continued excessively warm. After a hard march of twenty miles, we arrived late in the evening at the village where we expected to find the much-sought but little-loved rebels.

The citizens informed us that John Morgan's force of cavalry passed through there the day before, going north. Our command bivouacked there, and resumed the march early the 12th, over rough roads, through the hills northwest, thirteen miles, and we were in the village of Liberty.

Our brigade remained here until the next evening, living principally on green corn. The citizens here appeared to be more loyal than any we had found in Tennessee, displaying the stars and stripes as we marched through town. The loyal women here came out to our camp, and cheerfully loaned the soldiers their cooking utensils. This day's rest among these people, and the benefit of a good bath in the clear stream, which most of us enjoyed, greatly refreshed us in soul and body.

At 4 o'clock, p. m., the 13th, we again formed column, and, as usual, took the back track. The moon shone bright, and we halted at 10 o'clock at Smithville, and rested until morning. The officers and men of the Eighth about this time became very solicitous to be mounted, so we could have a chance to catch some of the rebel cavalry, for, said our men, we find it impossible to either head them off or catch them on foot.

We left Smithville at sunrise the 14th, and at 5 p. m. re-entered our camp at McMinnville. The following ten days, when not on picket or other duty, the time was spent in vigorous drilling. One evening, at dress parade, we were rejoiced to learn that General Nelson was relieved from the command, and would proceed immediately to Kentucky to take command of raw recruits then arriving at Louisville and Cincinnati. We did not envy those same raw recruits their pleasures in obeying the orders of their general. Though, with all Nelson's harsh, overbearing, and often wanton cruelty to his subordinates, he often did a good thing in protecting his soldiers from the grasping greed of sutlers or citizens, with whom our boys often traded. One day, before Nelson left us, a crowd of soldiers were collected around a lank-looking, long-haired Tennesseean, who bore on his arm a basket containing some tough-looking pies. Between the two thick crusts was a darker streak of woolly peaches. General Nelson came along the street, and noticing the citizen, stepped up, saying: "Here, my man, what have you there to sell?"

Citizen—"Pies, sar; unly fifty cents apiece, sar."

The general broke one open, and dropped it back in the basket, exclaiming, "Only fifty cents apiece!" Drawing his sword, he continued: "Now, you infernal, lecherous, spindle-shanked devil! those things wouldn't digest in the stomach of a hyena. How many have you?"

Citizen tremblingly replied: "Six, I b'leve."

General Nelson, raising his sword more threateningly, said: "Now, eat the last one in short order, or I'll cut your infernal head from your worthless carcass!" The poor, frightened fellow munched and swallowed in painful haste, until his eyes, which continuously watched the uplifted steel, assumed a frog-like prominence. Thus, he worried down over two dollars' worth of his dark, choky pastry. Nelson then ordered the would-be pie vender outside our pickets, telling him if he should ever see him here again on any pretext, death would certainly be his doom. We saw no more of that enterprising tradesman.

Brigadier General Ammon assumed command of the troops in and around McMinnville. The 24th August, we were ordered to prepare two days' rations, load the baggage and be ready to march at

1 o'clock, p. m. At that hour we were in column, and the general wish and belief was that we were leaving this "rebel hole" for the last time. The Eighth halted in the town to assist the division quartermaster to burn some old worn out tents and quartermaster stores that had been condemned as unserviceable. We came up with the main force at midnight, at the forks of the Tullahoma and Altamont roads. The next morning our little army was, by some misunderstanding of the guards and buglemen, permitted to sleep later than the general intended, consequently many of us ate our breakfast while on the march. Before noon we arrived at the foot of the mountain, on the Altamont road. Here the rebels had just passed over, and had obstructed the naturally difficult, narrow road by felling trees, and our artillery and wagons were completely blocked.

Our supply of rations was quite limited. A great deal of musket firing around the neighboring farms began soon after we halted. Officers and men knew there was no enemy on our side of the mountain except those unarmed, but they were often thought to not be entirely docile. One member of the Eighth came walking into camp, soon after the shooting began, with a quarter of mutton, and apologetically remarked to his captain: "Cap'n, I do respect General Buell's orders, but darn me ef a rebel sheep shall butt me." Judging from the quantity of roast and fried mutton consumed that evening in the division, especially by the Eighth Kentucky and

Thirty-fifth Indiana, people in that locality must have owned a goodly number of belligerent sheep.

The 26th, the whole division returned to our respective camps around McMinnville. drilling and picketing as before.

Some of the Thirty-fifth Indiana, on the 27th, went outside our picket lines and took possession of Mr. Argoe's apple and peach brandy distillery, and when found, a few days after, were doing a thriving business working off the tubs of bruised fruit on hand. When these modern "moonshiners" were brought up before Colonel Matthews for violation of orders and taking private property, Dennis McLew, the leader, when asked why he did so, replied : "Plaze yer honor, Colonel, but it wuz too bad, indade ; the cowardly spalpeen ov a ribel had taken himself away, and the paich mash wuz sphoilin intoirely ; an', yer honor, tho' I do say it myself, I'm the boy as can make the rale ould crayther as will warrum up the boys' stummicks before atein' the indacent food we get here in this haythen counthry." As some of the "boys" had taken too much of the "crayther," Colonel Matthews had the self-appointed distiller and a few others tied up until their stomachs cooled off a little.

CHAPTER V.

The 2d day of September, all the troops about McMinnville had orders to prepare to march, and early the 3d everything loyal to the United States was leaving this part of Tennessee. It was now an evident fact that the rebels in large force were invading Kentucky. Many of the most loyal citizens with their families joined our column, which was now raising clouds of dust on the Murfreesboro road. We bivouacked at Logan's Plains, where we joined General Wood's division. The 4th of September our column arrived at Bradyville, and the next day at 1 o'clock p. m. were once more in Murfreesboro. Here all the sick and those unable to march were ordered on the train for Nashville. About half a dozen officers of the Eighth, including myself, with a few of the Twenty-first Kentucky, got aboard the cars. If we were not all of us equally sick we were certainly about on an equality in present cash assets. At the Nashville depot, while we were holding a committee of the whole on our financial standing, the sight of our cheerful and accommodating sutler was a pleasant surprise to us. We instantly surrounded "Uncle Bob," and soon relieved him of his surplus cash, and once more were able to face an extortionate landlord or a frowning rebel landlady, and were soon registered on Mrs. Peace's books.

For several days our troops poured through the city northward in a living stream.

The 7th, late in the day, our command were passing through. Sick and feeble, as some of us were, we had no notion of being left in Dixie while the rebels were invading the " sacred soil " of Kentucky. Captains Powell and Thomas and the author being scarcely able to walk, had, through the assistance of Chaplain Paul, purchased a horse of a Union citizen at a very low price intending to try to keep up with our command by riding, each by turn. It was agreed that as I was the most feeble, I should have the first ride, while they with the others joined the column. I spent some time trying to find a saddle for sale cheap—one dollar being all the money we three had left after paying for our steed. I at last concluded to postpone the luxury of a saddle, and gave a grinning darkie twenty-five cents for an old bridle, threw my gum blanket and fatigue coat on Carlo's back, and mounted, with sword and pistols balancing my haversack across the withers of the horse. I made better time through the streets of the city than was agreeable to my aching bones. I overtook the regiment about 10 p. m. encamped near Edgefield Junction, on the Louisville pike. All the men were covered with dust, and their clothing badly worn, especially shoes and pantaloons. The men had been compelled to wear their underclothing so long without change that many of them had become infested with vermin—in army parlance called " graybacks." Our requisitions for clothing here were only partially filled, and orders were given to company commanders to issue only to those of their men that were in greatest need, and as about all were eager claimants for pants, the captains generally settled the matter by calling the company into line and passing along in the rear raised each man's coat skirts, and those whose pants had given out worst in the most embarrassing places, were ordered to step forward and received a new pair.

The 8th, our command moved a short distance up the pike and bivouacked for the night. Here Gen. T. L. Crittenden took command of the Twenty-first Army Corps, composed of the First, Second and Third Divisions, to the latter our brigade belonged, still commanded by Ammon.

The army was all life and bustle early the 9th. Canteens filled with water, and a fresh supply of forty rounds of cartridges in our cartridge boxes, we marched on the pike through Goodlettsville, then Quiet Hill, and halted for the night at Tyre Springs. Here a few more of our ragged boys received another partial supply of clothing. Before dark several of the Fifty-first Ohio and Eighth Kentucky boys had straggled off into the woods to hunt paw-paws, and were captured by a company of rebel cavalry within a half mile of camp. All our boys escaped except John Townsend, and he made his escape a few days after.

The 10th, our column moved on fourteen miles and halted near Mitchellsville at an old rebel rendezvous they called Camp Trouser. Here our brigade alone slaughtered fifteen beeves and over one hundred sheep, also a few porkers and many chickens were taken and dressed in a private manner. Private Carmoody, "our Irishman," remarked, "Faith an' we'd not be afther lavin' the State with lank haversacks or empty stomachs aither."

At 6 o'clock on the morning of the 11th, our columns were again in motion and soon passed the large stone in the road that indicated the State line. As the Eighth passed over the line the boys gave three lusty cheers. We were delayed several hours waiting for our long train of wagons to cross Sharp's Branch—the rebels having torn up the bridge. That evening we passed through the pretty town of Franklin, Ky. Here crowds of women had collected on porticos and in front yards and displayed several Union flags, causing loud and long cheering from the troops. We halted for the night within five miles of town.

On the following morning, orders were given by General Buell that, until further orders, only half rations would be issued to the troops of this command. The Third Division (from cause probably never known only to General Buell himself) was detained here two days; during that time the rebels had torn up portions of the L. & N. Railroad. The half ration order caused considerable foraging on an individual scale. Col. Barnes and other officers of the 8th remonstrated with the men against foraging in our native State. As the Colonel said, "setting a bad example for other State's regiments to follow."

But other troops did not wait for any bad examples to influence them when their half rations did not half satisfy their keen appetites. A flock of goats and a good-sized sweet potato patch had already contributed largely to supply the 35th's lacking half ration, and without following their example, our boys thought the immediate future not very promising for bounteous living, and our camp guards had been standing with their backs toward the aforesaid potato patch and had failed to heed the bleating of more than one goat in the corn near by. At last Chandler B., of Co. I, caught the old billy of all the billies in the corn. The old, bearded patriarch proved too stout for Chandler. He not daring to shoot, caught his prey by the horns. The goat, in its frantic efforts to regain freedom, came tearing through the regiment, our heroic forager holding on to the horns with the tenacity of "grim death to a dead African," sometimes on top the goat, at others being dragged on the ground by the muttering goat. The loud cheering of the men, nor the terrible oaths of the colonel did not make him break his hold, nor lose his determination for fresh meat. Thus the two re-entered the high corn where the guards soon found Chandler with a few of his more timid comrades taking off the goat's hide. Our conquering hero was marched to colonel's tent. Colonel B.—" Now, sir, give your reasons for this flagrant violations of my recent orders, and be d—d quick about it, too." Chandler—" Colonel, I never meant disrespect to you, but I see'd them durned

35 Irishers agoen fur the whole flock, and they'd killed all but that old tough devil. He run over to our side and by golly I was 'termined they shouldn't have him, an' I jist went fur 'em." This earnest explanation came near making the colonel relax his assumed sternness. Chandler was put on extra duty, but said extra rations made it all right.

The 12th a considerable skirmish took place one and a half miles east of us, between our cavalry and some of Forrest's rebels.

The 13th, we resumed the march, and late that evening halted within two miles of Bowling Green, at a large spring, issuing from a cave. In a short time that stream ran dirty soap suds, as thousands availed themselves of the opportunity to bathe and wash dirty shirts. One day's rations were issued, but was barely sufficient for one meal. The corn crop was just sufficiently soft to be easily grated into meal. Our men made graters of half canteens and every piece of old tin or sheetiron that could be found, and these were kept constantly in use while we were at a halt. The varied sounds of these many shapes and sizes of graters throughout a division made a noise that will long be remembered by surviving Union soldiers of this war. We remained here three days. The second day three days' full rations of damaged, wormy flour were issued, and the bacon was worse than the flour.

The 15th, we heard cannonading north of us, which we soon after learned was at Mumfordsville, Ky. The soldiers of our army, and especially our

Kentucky boys, were impatient at what we conceived to be useless delays, while the enemy were outstripping us in the race for the city of Louisville, and overrunning the best portion of the State. At 3 p. m., the 16th, the welcome bugle sounded, and we marched through town, crossed Green River on pontoons, halted and spent the night in sight of Bowling Green. The following morning the bugle sounded the assembly. At the first dawn of daylight, without breakfast, we formed column and marched quick-step for five miles. We halted half an hour at a filthy pond, where the men were allowed to fill their canteens with what they called "mule soup," as there were several dead carcasses lying putrifying in the water, probably intentionally placed there by the armed "Southern gentlemen." By 3 o'clock, p. m., we had put eighteen miles more behind us, without anything to eat since the previous night, and the commissary wagons far behind. Our boys were too tired to forage for something to eat, and it would have been a fruitless search, as we had now struck the recent track of the famishing rebel army. About 2 o'clock next morning the long looked for commissaries arrived, and everybody was aroused, in the midst of a hard shower of rain, to draw and cook one day's rations. Flour was issued, and as pans and other means of cooking were quite limited, we were being hurried into column while a great many of the men's "cakes were dough." We made a quick march to Bell's Tavern, seven miles north, where we expected to find a force of the enemy. We only found the telegraph wires cut, and some damage done to the railroad. A few miles further, and we made a halt until sunset. We then moved on up two miles to Cave City. The night was very dark, but soon the whole surrounding country was lighted by the blaze of our fence-rail fires. We drew three days' rations, with orders to cook them and be ready to march by early morning. The wormy flour was here cooked in all the known ways, and many ways hitherto unknown—at least to the writer. There were biscuits, slapjacks, pancakes, fried dough, and some placed the dough on the cleanest boards or flat pieces of rails, and propped it up johnny-cake style, while a great many roped the dough around sticks, which were kept constantly turning before the fire until cooked. After all, scarcely any of it could have been eaten in daylight by any other than soldiers or Digger Indians, as the numerous long worms one was forced to eat or pick out would not have much suited an epicure.

After all this night's hurry and worry we were not ordered to move from here for three days. This delay caused the men to swear and fret. Many of the officers now, as well as the men, began to swear that they believed General Buell did not want to press the enemy hard enough to bring on a general engagement; and from here on to Louisville, when there was a general halt, there were many such expressions as "What's up now?" "Nothing, only Bragg's got a wagon broken down, and old Buell's stopped to wait for him to get started." While at

Cave City, our cavalry and that of the enemy skirmished around ahead a little, which was repeated daily until we neared the Ohio River.

At last, after we had about disposed of our three days' cooked rations, the evening of the 21st September, we again took to the dusty road, and marched by midnight to Mumfordsville, fifteen miles; waded the river, waist deep, stacked arms and lay down, not feeling much like praising our general-in-chief for the discomforts of our wet clothing. Captains Hickman and Winbourn both had to be left here at a private house, being too sick to be carried in the ambulance further.

The 22d, before forming column, about forty rebel prisoners, picked up by our cavalry, passed south, being paroled. We halted at Bacon Creek for water, where another installment of paroled rebels met us. Our men cheered them, and said to each other: "May be we will get to fight the hungry, dirty rascals yet."

Late in the evening the whole command halted near Upton Station, having marched hard the most of the previous night and all day in dust, often six inches deep, causing a cloud almost suffocating, rendered less endurable by the scarcity of water to quench our famishing thirst. One day's rations were issued, with orders to cook and prepare for the next day. Water and wood both being scarce, or very inconvenient to get, the exhausted men generally fell down to sleep without converting their spoiled flour into bread. Consequently, on the sounding of the assembly the 23d, the majority of our division had only began to prepare breakfast. The most of the men crammed their uncooked dough and bacon into their haversacks, swearing at thus being hurried off. Some in their wrath unwisely threw away their flour or dough. From Upton Station until we halted in Louisville our command was scarcely given time to eat or sleep, as the main force of the enemy had been forced by our cavalry to turn off toward Lebanon and Bardstown.

Now commenced the race between us and the enemy for Louisville. By 2 o'clock, p. m., we marched twenty miles to Elizabethtown. Here we halted three hours, and cooked and eat of what little was left of the last night's issue, the majority being too exhausted to go to the fields to forage. At 5 p. m. the bugle's warning notes bid us get into column, and off again. Ten miles further, great numbers gave out with blistered feet, or were overcome from want of sleep, and dropped by the roadside, but before daylight all came up to where the main force had halted.

The morning of the 24th, we did not require much time to cook, as we had little or nothing left. When we arrived at West Point, at the mouth of Salt River, at one o'clock, p. m., we learned that Bragg's main force was at Bardstown, Ky. We crossed Salt River and stopped, three miles further on, on the southern bank of the Ohio River.

On the 25th of September, by a severe march of twenty-seven miles through the dust, which was for miles from six to eight inches deep, we arrived in the lower edge of the city of Louisville near midnight, our eyes and feet sore from the hot dust, and the hungriest, raggedest, tiredest, dirtiest, lousiest and sleepiest set of men the hardships of this or any other war ever produced. This was the general condition of all the troops that came through from Tennessee. The 27th, we moved out two miles from the city, on the Nashville pike, where our division washed up what clothing we had worth that trouble, drew new clothing, some camp equipage, with the promise of again obtaining sight of that important and ever welcome individual, the paymaster. Company commanders went to work, and many of us did not stop to sleep until the pay-rolls were ready for the men's signatures, as all the officers and men were without money. Those who had not spent nor sent their pay home, had been importuned by less prudent or less lucky comrades, and borrowed and spent about every greenback the regiment could command.

The 30th, the long looked-for paymaster appeared in our division, and paid off many of the troops. Our men were beginning to feel "bully," by the little rest, clean, new clothes and prospect of pay; and, to add to many of their jubilant feelings, some one came in from the city and reported that General Jeff. C. Davis had killed General Nelson for abusive language. No one considered Nelson a coward or friend to the enemy, but he was pronounced a tyrant of the "first water."

About this time all the oldest regiments in the army were desirous, and many of them clamorous, for General Thomas to supercede General Buell. Apparently all had lost that confidence in our general-in-chief that is so essential for the efficiency of troops.

We received general orders to leave all trunks,- officers' desks, company books and extra baggage at Louisville, and prepare to march in light order at 6 o'clock the next morning. The enemy's cavalry had been skirmishing with our advance pickets out ten or twelve miles southwest. Our men said: "Well, we would like to have a few more greenbacks, but we want to be led to the enemy." Many of the Eighth said: "That old poke-easy general of ours has allowed the thieving rebels to overrun the best portion of the State, and they are now in full possession of our homes. All we care for now is to be allowed to have a chance to thrash and drive the lousy devils out, or kill or capture the whole army of thieves, with all their long train of stolen goods."

CHAPTER VI.

The morning of the first day of October, 1862, was one of those bright, pleasant days so exhilerating after a few white frosts. With one day's grub and a full supply of cartridges, our brave, hardy boys, without a murmur for pay, cheerfully formed in column, and in quick time marched toward Bardstown, where we understood the main force of Bragg's army were. Now that we had succeeded in placing ourselves between the· enemy and our immense stores of supplies, every man appeared eager for battle. After marching eight miles, we heard the lively popping of carbines ahead. We broke into a double-quick, and in three miles further came to where the Fourth Indiana Cavalry and the rebels had a few minutes before been engaged in a skirmish. Our brigade was ordered to halt, front and cap every piece of ordinance. We then marched in line of battle to the brow of a hill as supports to the cavalry, but the Johnnies kept going on South, and again not an Eighth gun was fired at the enemy. As we filed off to bivouack for the night the men of the Eighth and Twenty-first Kentucky gave many expressions of disappointment. One of the Eighth shouted to the Twenty-first: "The thieving devils always serve us that way. They'll never stop long enough for us to get a shot at 'em.".

The Ninth Division (General Woods) passed us and formed the advance of our corps. We camped at Hays Springs, having made a short march. The Ninety-ninth Ohio, a new regiment only two weeks from their homes, was here added to our brigade, the 2d of October. Their new outfit and crowded knapsacks, with two wool blankets and new great coats neatly folded and strapped on top of knapsacks, contrasted strangely with the appearance of our boys, in light marching order, who had learned by sad experience not to make beasts of burden of themselves, carrying weighty articles that would not, probably, be needed for months.

The advance of General Woods' division continued to skirmish with the rear of the enemy's force, a few miles ahead of us, especial about Mount Washington. On the 3d, skirmishing for an hour was quite spirited. On that night we bivouacked on the south fork of Salt River. Here we drew and cooked three days' rations, expecting to engage in some sanguinary work with the rebels before we ate them, as it was reported the main force would certainly make a stand at Bardstown, eighteen miles southwest of us. Every man in the Eighth, at the sound of the assembly, with loud cheers, took their places in the column, eager to have a trial at short range with the invaders, but the evening of the 4th, on arriving near Bardstown, we learned with some regret that, after a little skirmishing with our advance, the enemy had fled toward Danville and Springfield. We began to think, from the uniform distance these two large bodies of belligerents kept apart, that neither commander-in-chief desired a general engagement.

The 5th and 6th October we made short marches, reaching Springfield, twenty miles, in two days' march. It now became evident to all that General Bragg had abandoned the scene of conflict. By somebody's management, or mismanagement, we were not ordered to march until near noon the 8th. During that forenoon Rousseau's, Gilbert's and Jackson's divisions, of McCook's corps, were hotly engaged with Bragg's main army, while here lay, scattered around within from two to eight miles, two whole corps of as brave, reliable troops as ever shouldered a musket, lying impatiently awaiting orders to move on the enemy. At last we received orders, and were only two hours in double-quicking to within supporting distance of our comrades—McCook's corps—who had by this time all become engaged, as also a part of the Fourth Corps, General Thomas. Up to 2 p. m. many had been slain on both sides. At 3 o'clock, just as we arrived within a mile of the engagement, only the artillery was playing freely. General Bragg led a ferocious charge in person on the center of our lines, where General Rousseau's division maintained its position, and hurled the tumultuous rebels back with complete success, our artillery plowing avenues of death through their serried columns, while the musketry mowed down whole ranks of "grey-backs" as they rolled frantically forward toward the federal lines. They were compelled to retire from that portion of the field in confusion, leaving the ground strewn with their dead, dying and wounded. But another charge, led by General Buckner, on General Jackson's division, met with better success, and exceeded in ferocity anything yet exhibited in the war. The overwhelming numbers of the enemy threw this division into disorder. Generals Jackson and Terrill both fell. Then Generals Sheridan and Mitchell's commands became engaged, and exhibited that heroism characteristic of western troops. But I cannot enter into further details of this bloody fight, as the author's designs are only to follow the fortunes of the Eighth Kentucky. Thus the battle raged, indecisively, with only a part of our forces engaged, and our whole corps ready, willing and waiting, within supporting distance, like eager greyhounds straining at the leash, praying and pleading to be led on to support our brave, battling comrades. But no orders came. Brigade and regimental commanders, like their men, were instantly expecting orders and ever ready to spring forward at the word. At sunset the battle merged into an artillery duel, and as darkness spread its sable mantle over these sanguinary scenes, the Union army reposed upon their arms. During the night the enemy leisurely resumed his retreat.

The loss in Rousseau's division alone was nineteen hundred killed and wounded. In all the other troops the loss was about four thousand killed, wounded and prisoners. The enemy's loss was only a little more than the federal, proving little more than a drawn battle.

On the morning of the 9th, when it became known that Bragg's whole army had retreated south, with his long train of well loaded wagons, the general feeling of chagrin and disgust was truly great. Said our men, "After all our hard marching and bad living, we had rather met with defeat in battle than to have let the enemy slip off with their spoils without more severe punishment." Many officers and men openly expressed their doubts of General Buell's fidelity. Some of the men swore if we could not have a better department commander they would send the present one to "happy Canaan after Nelson." The intelligent reader will not wonder at the ill feeling of the Kentucky soldiers when he is reminded that Bragg's long train contained fifteen hundred wagon loads of provisions, clothing and other necessaries for his army, together with several thousand horses and beeves, and an immense amount of groceries and goods, gathered from the principal towns of Kentucky, and now, in all probability, they would make a safe retreat in possession of all this plunder. Buell had only engaged the enemy once within five months, and then against his wish. Thus, Bragg had been allowed to traverse the richest portions of our native State, almost undisturbed; to even perpetrate the fraud of inaugurating a governor at Frankfort; to rob, defraud and terrify the Union citizens and our friends in one of the most populous States in the Union; and was now about to make his escape, almost without interference. This was more than the furious, patriotic temper of our mountain boys could endure. It is not singular, after all this, that the federal government removed General Buell the same month (October), and appointed General Wm. S. Rosecrans in his stead; but not in time for the latter to inflict any of the well-deserved punishment the willing troops desired to give the rebels.

The 9th we moved up and bivouacked on the east side of Perryville. The 10th our brigade moved out near Harrodsburg, and on the morning of the 11th some rebel cavalry made a dash at our picket lines, but were sent off in a hurry by a well directed fire. None of our regiment received any wounds.

The 12th, our brigade marched in line of battle towards Dicks River, over some very fine bluegrass farms for miles. We left a number of fences leveled as we advanced by right of companies to the front. Some of the brigade once came in sight of a small detachment of rebel cavalry, with whom a few shots were exchanged. At night we bivouacked near Camp Dick Robison, on Dick's River, where we learned a large body of the enemy had just left. The 13th we marched into Danville, the county seat of Boyle County, near which place we bivouacked. The people generally, being loyal, made many demonstrations of joy at being once more delivered from rebel rule, by waving numerous flags. We were preparing our evening meal, when we heard skirmishing ahead. Colonel Wolford's cavalry had stirred up a few of the enemy's rear guard. Our regiment was instantly into column and double-quicked four miles out to support Wolford, and try, as the boys said, "to get a few shots at them Johnnies." They had cleared out before we arrived. We returned to camp, drew two days' rations, and received orders to be ready to move at 6 o'clock next morning. At that hour we took up our pursuit, with all the division, on the Crab Orchard road. We halted for the night at Stanford. About midnight we were all aroused and into line, and in five minutes were in column double-quicking out toward Crab Orchard, to support the Thirty-fifth Indiana, who, being on advance picket, were fired on by the enemy's rear guard pickets. Three miles from Stanford we found the Thirty-fifth, who had discovered the enemy's camp fires half a mile from them, at the bridge over Sugar Creek. We had two pieces of artillery, with which we threw a few shells at the fires and then advanced, but the rebels had made a hasty retreat, leaving us sundry skillets and pots, containing their now smoking pones of corn bread and meat, which we relished for our breakfast, notwithstanding it was somewhat over-cooked. Some of the Eighth boys found a sleeping rebel in a barn near by. From him we learned that we were not far behind the rebels' long wagon train, consequently there was skirmishing occasionally all day, and our artillery was constantly shelling the timbered districts ahead. We did not halt for the night until 9 o'clock. The Eighth was placed half a mile in advance of the division on picket near the town of Mount Vernon, but everything was quiet except a lumbering noise to the southward, which proved the enemy felling trees to prevent or impede our pursuit.

The 16th we halted near Rock Castle River, and sent forward heavy details to cut and clear the obstructions from the Wild Cat Mountain road. On the 18th, the Eighth Kentucky, under Lieutenant Colonel May, was ordered out on a scout near the "Big Hill," where the regiment about dark succeeded in surprising and capturing forty of Chenault's new rebel cavalry and thirteen good horses. Had it not been for the eagerness of a few of Company A, firing before orders, we would have bagged the principal part of that regiment, who were about to dismount and camp for the night. All those yet on their horses made a precipitate retreat, while those who had tied their horses were left *hors de combat*, and surrendered. The Eighth then returned that night with their prisoners to Mount "Wild Cat," where we remained until midnight of the 21st. We returned to near Mt. Vernon, and on the 22d passed through that place. There we took the direct road toward Somerset, bivouacked within thirteen miles of the latter, and arrived there the evening of the 23d.

The Kentucky troops began to think a little pay from Uncle Sam would be in order. We had many married men in the command who had not heard a word from their families for three or four months, and knowing that had the invading rebels left them unmolested, the cold weather was beginning, and admonished them to try and send their anxious, loving wives and children a few dollars, to make them somewhat comfortable for the winter. We had passed by our home (or the majority had), without a murmur; but now tidings began to reach them by loyal fathers and friends just from home, who, being anxious to see sons or brothers, began to overtake us, that in many instances Union families had been stripped by the invaders of what little some of them had, and in many instances entering their houses and taking all their meat, cutting out and carrying off cloth from the loom, that the frugal soldier's wife had toiled to spin and weave to clothe their dependent little ones. There being in Kentucky no organized relief for poor soldiers' wives and children, as was the case in more Northern States, and in the terror and excitement of the presence of the two great contending armies every one at home appeared to think that seeing after the safety and comforts of his own was all that patriotism or selfishness required. These well confirmed rumors made many of the married men of the Eighth and Twenty-first Kentucky consider the probable condition of their dependent families. But on the 28th the column formed without complaint, and many sad faces and anxious hearts were moving on further from the loved ones at home, who needed the long expected pay. The snow had fallen several inches deep, and the young timber bent over our road with the unshed foliage weighted with wet snow. Our supply train had been sent on to Columbus, in Adair county, thirty-six miles from Somerset. We were two days in reaching there. Our rations were there, but the long promised paymaster again disappointed us, and a good many of the men began to complain bitterly about their pay. Col. Barnes called the line officers together and asked us to persuade the men to refrain from any words or actions that might bring the command into disgrace. The Company commanders collected their faithful soldiers around them and readily admitted their wrongs and grievances to be such, but that we now had a commander who would, when appealed to on their behalf, not only have them paid but would, on the colonel's request, grant the men who had families short furloughs. After this advice, and Col. B. saying he would use his influence to obtain furloughs for the married men, the 1st day of November the boys shouldered their muskets with more cheerfulness, saying: "We will still do our duty and see if this new general will not do us justice, and give us a chance to fight a little instead of wearing our bodies and patience out trotting around after the enemy without getting a chance to fire a gun."

The brigade marched thirteen miles and bivouacked on a large creek. Our sutler overtook us and sold out one load of goods to the men, on credit, of course.

The evening of the 2d our camp fires lighted up the banks of Beaver creek, within three miles of the town of Glasgow. We passed through that place the next morning and camped on the Louisville pike, four miles from town.

Here we met the balance of our corps, and were paid on the 4th by Major Nunes up to the last of August.

The principal topic in the Eighth were the married men's promised furloughs. Col. Barnes appealed to General Crittenden in behalf of his married soldiers, but without success. When this became known that evening (the 4th), there was some excitement, and many unjust imprecations privately heaped on our well-meaning colonel, whose wife, in company with Captain Thomas' wife and Mrs. and Mr. Creed had arrived in camp to see their husbands. The men, in their bitterness and disappointment, swore that the colonel and some of the other officers did not care, so they could see their families, while theirs were not able to visit them. That night several companies of the Eighth and Twenty-first did not get quiet before midnight. Next morning there were quite a number out of those regiments absent. Their officers knew very well that those men had not deserted, but chafing under the circumstances and their real and imaginary wrongs, had determined at all hazards to see their families and leave them some money and return. I will here state that nearly every one did, and by their officers making long and earnest petitions to the corps and division commanders to have those men reinstated without loss of pay and allowances, succeeded, and after, as before, they were the best of soldiers, many of them only remaining at home a few days, others probably two weeks. Fifty men thus absented.

The 5th of November we resumed the march south. Halted for the night on the barren fork of Green river. On the 6th arrived at Scottsville, the county seat of Allen county, thirty miles from Glasgow. The 7th we re-crossed the State line and bivouacked in Tennessee. As we passed over the supposed line our regiment gave three cheers. One man in Company A, at the head of the column, shouted out: "We buys no more chickens." Some one else replied, " No, not of rich rebels! but, boys, spare the poor." Many voices were raised, " that's right!" " but we guard no more d—n rebel's cornfields and hen roosts." Three cheers were given for old Kentucky and the Union. We spent a wet, snowy night, by large log fires.

The 8th we arrived at Gallatin, Tennessee, and camped two miles south of town, on the bank of the Cumberland river.

The 9th our men did a big day's washing of clothes, as some of them said, " If it is Sunday." At this time the men absent from the Eighth outnumbered those present for duty, a large percentage having been left sick at Nashville, Louisville, and Danville, Kentucky. With the late absentees made the number of fighting men present less than 300.

CHAPTER VII.

At one o'clock, on the morning of the 10th of November, the regiments in the Third Brigade were aroused from their slumbers by the adjutants quietly passing around to the company commanders, saying: "Captain, get your men ready to march in ten minutes, without noise." Tent flies and blankets were hastily rolled up and piled into wagons, with cooking utensils, and in less than thirty minutes the brigade was silently crossing the Cumberland, on a temporary tressel foot bridge. We were trying to slip up on John Morgan's two thousand rebs at Lebanon. We had learned the importance of keeping our movements from the knowledge of the people of Middle Tennessee, and the only noise made was the unavoidable sound of our feet. We halted at daylight, ate a hastily prepared breakfast and off again, every man in the brigade keeping his place and number with a promptness that would be commendable on a holiday drill.

There were very many very sore feet in the command. But with determination and cheerfulness beaming in every face, we hurried along the dusty stone road. Our advance guard came on to the rebel pickets within a mile of Lebanon. A well directed fire from our men brought one of the Johnnies down, and the others of the squad fired off their pieces into the air as they fled toward town, leaving their wounded comrade. We quickened our pace and entered the deserted town at 9 a. m., the enemy having made a disorderly retreat down the Murfreesboro road. Our men were not idle the six hours we remained here. A large lot of flour, bacon and whisky fell into our hands. As we had no means of transportation, Col. Matthews gave orders to press every wagon, mule, horse and buggy that could be found. All who were not engaged in collecting this novel forage train, were put to cooking the flour into bread. Our men not being very well supplied with utensils, the majority of the Eighth boys paid many of the poorer class of citizens liberally in flour to convert a large portion of that article into bread. All the whisky, except two barrels, the colonel wisely destroyed by knocking out the heads and letting the contents flow on the ground. But, by some means, a considerable quantity of the "precious" fluid leaked into many canteens. Carmoody, "our Irishman," said, "'dade, 'an it's wicked we are, to be wastin' the pure ould stuff; but thin, them thavin' gorreelas 'l be dry es a fish when they come stalein' back."

Having accomplished all we could, at 6 o'clock p. m. our column formed behind our captured commissaries, drawn by old broken-down horses, that had seen hard service under Morgan's men. Vehicles of all kinds, except good ones, were in the train, driven principally by citizens, whose anxiety for the safe return of the pressed teams prompted them to volunteer their services. The men's haversacks were crammed full of smoking bread, and yet we had not room to store the large quanties which remained, but Captain Wilson, on the eve of leaving Lebanon, spied a buggy that had been overlooked. This was soon loaded, and the men of Companies C and H drew it along, in the ranks, by turns. All were in jubilant spirits, and marched up briskly on our return toward Nashville. About the middle of the night we came up with the Twenty-first Corps, at Silver Springs, having marched thirty-five miles in the last twelve hours—the last fifteen miles with extra loads, which made all of us enjoy that refreshing sleep none but the weary know how to appreciate.

We remained at Silver Springs six days, being the longest halt we had made for near three months. The rain fell in such quantities that drilling had to be dispensed with, and we were allowed to rest and enjoy full rations, with occasionally the luxury of a taste of our captured whisky, for a few mornings.

On the 13th the Eighth formed the guards to escort a forage train into the country, to collect forage while the wagons were being loaded. Our boys did not forget their own creature comforts, for on their return to camp nearly every man brought a little donation for his particular mess, such as a chicken, or a few potatoes; also, a good sized pumpkin graced the bayonet of nearly every gun.

At noon, the 17th, the regiment formed, and marched as guards to a supply train going to the Fourteenth Brigade, under Col. Hawkins, stationed at Rural Hill, twelve miles southeast of Silver Springs. The camp and garrison of our regiment were left in charge of the few men not able for duty, and after a tedious, muddy march, arrived late in the night and took up quarters on an old Methodist camp meeting ground, situated one-fourth of a mile from the brigade, the old plank shanties affording good protection from the drizzling rain, which had not ceased when we awoke early the morning of the 18th of November. The surrounding country was shrouded in a smoky mist. The 8th boys were within the shanties busily preparing and eating our morning meal, when we were a little surprised to hear a few of the 14th pickets fire and immediately after about two hundred rebel cavalry came charging toward our shanties yelling like savages, evidently unaware of our sheltered position. The officers and men of the 8th did not fool away any time to form in line, but every man seized his gun, choosing each his window or crack, while some knocked off boards for port-holes. On came the yelling Johnnies. When within easy range of the innocent looking shanties, Col. May gave the command, "Steady boys, fire." The volley that was poured into those unsuspecting Johnnies emptied so many saddles, they checked up in great confusion, and before they could realize their situation the deadly popping of our guns began again with such telling effect, the enemy were glad to retreat as fast as they came, leaving seven of their comrades dead and wounded on the field. A number of their wounded were carried off with the retreating party. In the pockets of a rebel lieutenant were found several "rat-tail" files, that some of their wounded acknowledged were to be used in spiking the artillery belonging to the Fourteenth Brigade, which were situated rather too far from the infantry for ready support. As soon as the disconcerted rebels were well out of sight and hearing our men stacked arms and began hunting up their scattered cooking utensils, and proceeded to finish their breakfast.

When the firing of the pickets were first heard by us, Lieutenant S—— seized one of the idle guns, at the same time was frantically urging his company to get into line. Little Ab. Wiseman, of Company K, ran up to Lieutenant S——, holding out his cup of coffee, saying: "Lieutenant, if you are not going to use my gun, just hold my coffee, and watch me tumble one of them jips." Wiseman made good use of his gun. After the action he asked the lieutenant what he had done with his coffee. The lieutenant had forgotten. "Well, lieutenant," said Ab., "you may do to trust in a fight, but you can't hold coffee for me again, sure."

Colonel Hawkins complimented the Eighth for their timely and efficient services, and, expecting another visit from the enemy, detained the regiment here until the next day, the 19th, when the regiment marched toward Nashville, and bivouacked near Stone river, and on the 20th moved two miles down the stream to the crossing of the Lebanon pike, where our convalescents and camp equipage, with the remainder of the brigade, had moved. The next day we crossed to the north side of the river, and laid off a regular camp near the Nashville and Lebanon pike.

The quartermaster issued to us some clothing that requisitions had been sent in for at Gallatin. Burnham was a man we all liked, but like many good men, he let strong drink too often get the better of him, and he resigned. Lieutenant Thos. Carson was appointed acting quartermaster.

Lieutenants W. Park and Jackson, with two men from each company, were here detached and assigned to the Mechanic's Corps.

The 24th, being a nice day, the Eighth drilled and had dress parade for the first time since the first of September. Colonel May made the regiment one of his interesting speeches. Some of our men that had been left sick in Nashville rejoined the command, and Sergeant Lewis, Company H, was appointed regimental wagonmaster.

The 25th we loaded up and marched across to the Murfreesboro pike, where we remained until the 28th. On that evening we moved near the deaf and dumb asylum, four miles south.

The regiment, as well as all the brigade, worked hard the 29th, clearing off brush and trying to arrange our old, leaky tents and flies, so as to protect us from the cold wind, that began to have an icy tinge. Here Captains Winbourn and Hickman rejoined us, both having been sick, and had been absent nearly two months.

The 1st day of December the Third Division was reviewed by General Rosecrans, not merely as a military custom, but to see the actual condition of his army. The men returned to camp much pleased with "Old Rosy." As he slowly passed along the line he was sure to notice any and all unsoldierly appearance. An untied shoe, or a badly adjusted knapsack, was mildly pointed out; if the fault appeared to be the neglect of the soldier, he would stop and administer a short but pointed good-humored lecture, often saying: "My men have to be clothed and fed if it takes the last dollar the government can raise to do it with. Now, boys, if you need pants, shoes or anything allowed the soldier, get after your captain; let the captain get after the quartermaster, and let him get after the brigade and division quartermasters, until the complaint reaches the quartermaster general, and our needs supplied; then, by the help of God, we will put down this rebellion." The old saying that "first impressions are lasting ones" proved true in this case. "Old Rosy" was ever after loved and respected by the men of our brigade, and his orders were at all times our law, and obeyed with cheerful alacrity.

The weather continued cold for several days, and our men suffered for want of overcoats. On the 7th of December Colonel Barnes left for Kentucky on leave of absence, but before he started he did a good act in calling Chaplain Paul to account for speculating off the men, by buying up at a very small per cent. all of the first issue of greenbacks, or demand notes, that were at all times worth their face in gold. He soon after sent in his resignation as chaplain of the Eighth, and it was accepted. " Timothy " had not proved of much advantage spiritually to the Eighth. But all the fault may not have been his. He had preached but few sermons, for the boys generally believed, from his general conduct, that he was not spiritually minded.

The 9th of December the Third Brigade and fifty wagons went out on Stone river, near Dobbin's Ferry, on a foraging expedition. The rebel cavalry had on several occasions attacked our foraging parties, and Colonel Matthews had two pieces of artillery taken along with us. Passing outside our outer videttes, we were soon near the ferry, on what we termed neutral ground. The Twenty-first and Eighth Kentucky proceeded to load the wagons from full cribs of corn on two adjoining farms. The Fifty-first Ohio and Thirty-fifth Indiana formed a good chain of pickets. We had been engaged in loading but a short time before a regiment of rebel cavalry made an attack on the Thirty-fifth, and for fifteen minutes the fighting was sharp, the Thirty-fifth being reinforced by the Fifty-first and part of the Twenty-first Kentucky, caused the Johnnies to fall back, leaving three of their men dead and several badly wounded. The Thirty-fifth lost three killed and sixteen wounded, principally slight, Adjutant Mullen being the first to fall, with a ball through his fair temple. The train was at last loaded and put in motion, Colonel Matthews, with the Thirty-fifth and Fifty-first, in front, the Twenty-first deployed, marched along by the wagons, and the Eighth commanded by Lieutenant Colonel May, forming the rear guard. A few stray shots fell among us from a body of mounted rebs on the opposite side of the river; but we knew that was done to attract our attention while a part of their force endeavored to cut us off from the train. The adjutant being absent, Colonel May asked me to mount a mule and act to him in that capacity. A half mile from the ferry the road ran through a dense growth of low cedars. Here we were attacked by two regiments of rebel cavalry on our left. We halted, fronted and opened a deadly oblique fire, our front rank kneeling to obtain clear range under the cedar boughs and give the rear rank better opportunity to fire low, and thus for twenty minutes we held them in check and did them serious injury. By Colonel May's order I went down the road a short distance and discovered part of the enemy's force were moving toward the rear of the train, evidently with the intention of trying to cut us off. I hurried back and reported to Colonel May that fact. He gave the command right face, forward, double quick, march, for one-fourth of a mile, and we came opposite the last named force, who were now dismounted. Again we halted, and returned their sharp fire, each man firing about four rounds. Seeing the danger of having our little regiment surrounded by such superior number, our brave old colonel's voice again rang out above the rattle of musketry, " Right face, forward, double quick, march!" Our column crowded the narrow road, Colonel May and myself being on the side of the column and mounted, were compelled to fall in to the rear of the regiment, and became special targets for the enemy, who came pressing on after us, after the boys cleared the road, the colonel and the author followed on. I was minus a cap, that had been shot from my head. The Colonel's overcoat had two bullet holes in it, and one through old Black's ear. We double-quicked in an oblique direction through the woods, and soon came to the other regiments, who had with our two pieces of artillery started back to assist us, while the wagon train went lumbering on safe into camp. The Eighth took position on the left of the brigade, the solid shot from the rebel battery whizzing uncomfortably near our heads. We lay in line, supporting our two pieces, until the last charge in the caissons were fired. The enemy appeared not to desire any more close work with small arms, and as night came on they fell back, and we marched back to our encampment. Our loss in the Eighth was two killed, fourteen wounded and five prisoners. Of the wounded were Lieut. McDaniel, slight wound in shoulder; private Ross, Company G; Fillpot and Corporal Landrum, Company A; one of Company C, one of Company I, and private B. Frailey, Company H, badly. Surgeon Mills amputated Landrum's arm the morning of the 10th. He and Frailey soon after died of their wounds. The enemy's loss was reported by the detail who went with flag of truce to bury our dead, to have been more than twice our loss, where we were first engaged. It would be unjust in me to mention any particular or individual act of bravery, when all nobly did their duty. The evening of the 10th our whole division moved back two miles nearer Nashville, where all remained until the 25th, the Eighth doing their share of forage and picket duty.

The 14th the author received an order from General VanCleve, now commanding the division, to proceed to Louisville and bring forward all the officers' desks and trunks, belonging to the Eighth, stored there; also, to collect and bring to the front all men there in hospitals or barracks belonging to the Third Brigade. Lieutenant McDaniel accompanied me to Nashville. Next morning I took the train for Louisville, where, by the 23d, I had collected twenty-eight men of our brigade, had the officers' baggage carted to the depot and put on the train that was to follow the one myself and men occupied. We arrived at Nashville before daylight, the 24th, that being the last train that passed over the road for several weeks, Morgan's guerrillas having on that night destroyed a portion of the road behind us.

At 8 o'clock I procured a pass for Sergeant Elkin and the men to get out through the pickets and sent them on to the command. I remained in the city until the next day, waiting for our baggage, when I learned by telegraph that the train containing our trunks was safe at Elizabethtown awaiting repairs to the road.

CHAPTER VIII.

By the 26th December, 1862, General Rosecrans had, by incessant labor, accumulated a large supply of quartermaster stores, and put the reorganized Army of the Cumberland in the best possible trim. He did not wait for clear weather, but early that rainy morning had the army all in motion on the several roads leading south from Nashville. The tents and camp and garrison equipage were left behind in charge of convalescents. Every soldier and officer, in light marching order, moved on through the incessant rain, which before night thoroughly soaked their clothing; but, with unabated courage, every man was careful to "keep his powder dry." On that dark, rainy night I came up with the Eighth, bivouacked in the cedars north of Lavergne.

A few days previous Captains Powell, Company B, and Wilson, Company C, with Lieutenants Gumm and McDaniel, Company I, had been granted permission, and had returned to Kentucky on leave of absence; and Captains Jamison, Company D, and Winbourn, Company H, and Lieutenant Neal, were left sick at Nashville. This reduced our line officers considerably, and, Company D having no commissioned officer present, Colonel May, now in command, put the author temporarily in command of that company. The other companies were commanded as follows:

Company A—Second Lieutenant Jacob Phips.
Company B—Second Lieutenant Joseph Blackwell.
Company C—First Lieutenant Wm. Park.
Company E—Captain Robert B. Hickman.
Company F—Captain John B. Banton.
Company G—Captain Landrum C. Minter.
Company H—First Lieutenant Wade B. Cox.
Company I—Lieutenant Newton Hughes.
Company K—Captain Henry Thomas.

Skirmishing commenced at early dawn the 27th, and increased into a sharp battle. As we advanced on Lavergne, at 8 o'clock, our shells soon set the town on fire, and two hours after, as our brigade passed through, the majority of the houses were in smoking ruins. The enemy gave way and fell back across Stewart's Creek, within ten miles of Murfreesboro. Near dark we bivouacked in the cedars just north of Stewart's Creek. The Eighth Kentucky did not have time to kindle their fires before we were ordered on picket, one-half the command on the line at a time. The rain had been pouring down all the afternoon, and our clothing, which was wet to the skin, felt anything but comfortable to a supperless man. We were not disturbed by the enemy throughout this disagreeable night, which at last gave way to a bright, pleasant morning. Being Sunday, our good Catholic general did not move his army, and all of us who were not detailed for forage and picket duty had a quiet rest.

The rebel pickets, though in easy hailing distance of ours, kept very quiet, and, in some instances relaxed their sullenness enough to indulge in a friendly chat with our pickets. This privates' armistice resulted in a squad from each belligerent army laying down their arms and advancing to the creek. Thus separated by the stream, the following conversation ensued:

Rebel—"What command does you-ens belong to?"

Federal—"The Third Brigade."

Rebel—"Who commands that ar brigade?"

Federal—"Colonel Matthews. What is your command?"

Rebel—"We ar Wheeler's; an' I believe you-ens are the fellers we fit at Dobbins' Ferry."

Federal—"You bet we are! What did you think of us?"

Rebel—"Darned good marksmen; but whar yer fellers tryin' to go ter?"

Federal—"To Murfreesboro."

Rebel—"Well, you-ens 'll find that ar a mighty bloody job, sho."

After an exchange of newspapers, thrown over by attaching to them a stone, each party retired to their posts.

During the night the rebels fell back, and early the 29th our division moved over the creek, and thence through farms, meeting no opposition except very tall cedar rail fences. We could hear heavy skirmishing on the Franklin road. At sunset we halted near Stone River, within two miles of Murfreesboro, where our engineers and mechanics were in a sharp skirmish with rebel sharpshooters. The former were trying to construct a bridge over the river near the Nashville Pike. The division formed line of battle in supporting distance of the pickets, who became quiet as darkness spread her sable curtain over the earth. We lay on our arms, ready for any night attack. The bare earth in the trampled-down cornfield was wet and cold, and but few men could feel comfortable enough to sleep.

The 30th day of December, 1862, passed without a general engagement. Both armies appeared to be feeling around with their skirmishers. Occasionally a sharp rattle of musketry would ring out through the cedars, caused by our lines crowding their pickets, especially in the afternoon. As the atmosphere was heavy with considerable fog and misty rain, the pickets on our right ran against those of the enemy, and a sharp battle for half an hour was the result. Then darkness again covered the two armies that now lay here confronting each other, only awaiting the light of day to enable them to engage in a mighty conflict of arms, that was destined to have great influence in deciding the future destiny of this great, free government.

Our division, after dark, formed column by division, and lay again in the open field. The rain ceased, and the wind shifted around from a cold quarter, making us feel sadly the need of a blanket, but no complaints were made by any one. Each man received sixty rounds of fresh cartridges, and laid down, expecting to engage in bloody work as soon as morning should appear.

In order that the reader may better understand subsequent events in this battle, we will give the order in which our army of 47,000 was placed. The Union line of battle extended in the form of an arc. The left of our division rested at a ford on Stone River, one mile west of the Nashville Railroad, and was the left of the line. The right wing lay near the Franklin Pike, and was composed of McCook's corps—Johnson's, Sheridan's and Davis' divisions. General Thomas' corps occupied the center, and consisted of Negley's and Rousseau's divisions, while General T. L. Crittenden's corps, composed of Woods' Palmer's and VanCleve's divisions, formed the left.

About daylight, the last day of the year 1862, our brigade, now under command of Colonel Price, of the Twenty-first Kentucky, was ordered, and double-quicked to the above named ford on our left. We waded the river, waist deep, the water being cold enough to make one catch his breath as it reached the hips. We hurried into line of battle in sight of the rebel pickets, and advanced on them about one-fourth of a mile. The Johnnies made the bullets sing over our heads as they fell back from our skirmish line, who gave them back a sharp fire. During this maneuver the firing on the extreme right had increased to a heavy battle. The constant roar of artillery and ominous crashing, rattle of small arms, told us plainly that the rebels were making a desperate attempt to turn our right wing. We were ordered to fall back and re-cross the river. The

Third Brigade, including the Eighth, formed a reserve line of battle near the ford, while the remainder of the division was ordered on to support the right, which was now evidently being pushed back by the combined force of three rebel corps—McCoun's, Cheatham's and Claiborne's. Johnson's command had first given way. The exultant rebels, partially intoxicated on whisky and gunpowder, followed up. Davis' division was next compelled to fall back. This left Sheridan's right exposed, which the rebels soon took advantage of. After standing the shock of the now furious foe for some time, they in turn were hurled back toward the center, where old "Lion-Heart" Thomas was riding back and forth in front of his lines of sturdy heroes, encouraging them. All the available force that could be taken from the left was concentrated here to reinforce the center, our little brigade being all that was left to watch the left wing. These were terrible moments. The horrible spectacle of thousands of our comrades fleeing before the enemy, a continuous stream of stretchers, bearing bleeding, torn and mangled bodies, coming back through our ranks, made our hearts quiver with sympathy for our bleeding comrades. But all interests were centered just then in the right center, and our boys chafed at being compelled to stand inactive and witness the fight and misery. The enemy, in heavy columns, emerged from the cedars, exulting in the belief that victory was theirs. The long line of blue-coats was still. The word of command was at last given. A dazzling sheet of flame burst from the blue ranks, which riddled the thick mass of the enemy. This was quickly followed by the roar of our artillery, shaking the earth and crushing into fragments whole regiments of grey-coats. Then the tide of battle turned, and the enemy was driven back over one mile, leaving the ground covered with their dead and dying. Mixed and mingled was the blood of the slain of both armies. General VanCleve, our division commander, was wounded, and Colonel Sam. Beaty took command of the division.

During the battle, a regiment of rebel cavalry made a dash at the house near the ford, used as a hospital. Our brigade charged down to the river bank and gave them a volley, and the one battery left with us gave them a few solid shot, that made them scamper back, leaving our doctors and wounded unmolested.

The battle ceased at 5 p. m., with our army considerably worsted. That night, at "Rosy's" headquarters, all the corps generals were assembled in council. General Rosecrans asked the starred crowd what he should do. General Crittenden said: "We may be able yet to whip the enemy here, general." Rosecrans, bringing his fist down on the table with much force, said: "Yes, and we will, if we have to fight them one week and live on parched corn all that time."

The Eighth spent this frosty night on the skirmish line near the river bank, above the ford. The rebel pickets showed no disposition to advance, and our orders were not to fire unless they did, the stream being between us. The night passed in comparative silence except the groans and shrieks of the wounded laying in the hospitals.

At 3 o'clock p. m. the heavy booming of the cannon ceased. Then we discovered the immense columns of the enemy moving toward us. They made a grand scene, moving over the wide, undulating field, with their numerous bright flags unfurled and fluttering in the wind, their several generals mounted on magnificent chargers, surrounded by their staff officers. This scene presented to my mind one of those sublime spectacles of the pomp of war, which form the bright, delusive side of a picture, in which horror, misery and death sadly predominated. On they came, regiments in close column by division. Our little isolated brigade, that "Old Rosy" had placed out as a bait to lure on the enemy into his well arranged trap, ordered in their skirmishers, but not until the brave and gallant Captain Banton and several of his men had fallen. For a few minutes our line was as still as the grave, but it was only the calm that preceeds the storm. A small elevation immediately in front concealed the mighty host of well disciplined grey coats from view for a few minutes. The gallant old Fifty-first Ohio on our right on higher ground opened their crashing sheet of fire first, then as the heads of the advancing enemy re-appeared within eighty rods of the 8th, our sturdy mountain boys received the anxiously desired order, "fire by file, fire." A blaze of fire and smoke ran along down our ranks, every

After the word "hospitals," at end of paragraph on page 128, read:

Early on New Year's morning our brigade waded the river. The water, about hip deep, was very cold to our already chilled legs. We hurried into line and advanced on the enemy's pickets, driving them from the timber into a large field. At the edge of this wood we halted and maintained our position; but the rebel pickets and sharp-shooters made it risky to stand erect, as the pickets kept up an irregular popping throughout the day, and we were not sorry when darkness permitted us to send details to the rear and prepare coffee. We suffered during the night on our regimental bed of weeds, as our blankets had been cheerfully donated to the wounded.

The 2d, before the sun appeared from behind the dark-green cedars, picket firing was resumed followed by heavy artillery all along the lines. Our advanced position made us an especial target for their artillery, while the skirmish balls kept up that ominous singing. Before noon several of Companies B and F had fallen on the picket line, and Shepherd, Company C, was killed; others were wounded by the enemy's shell, and our flag-staff was shivered by a solid shot.

being between us. The night passed in comparative silence except the groans and shrieks of the wounded laying in the hospitals.

At 3 o'clock p. m. the heavy booming of the canman taking a deliberate aim. The effect of this murderous fire became visible to all our men, which infused them with fresh courage. True, our brave lads were falling fast, but the enemy was checked and not a mounted rebel in sight of our line. Company commanders walked along behind their men with encouraging words and to "shoot low." The brave old "thirty-fives" on our left were also doing nobly. The ground on top of the ridge in our front was in fifteen minutes covered with dead, dying and wounded rebels, and many of our men were falling by the terrible fire of the enemy, who now began to work around to the right of the Fifty-first Ohio with an overwhelming force. At the same time another large force of the enemy were completely flanking the Thirty-fifth Indiana. The enemy were not more than forty steps in our front when we received the order to fall back, which we were compelled to do, leaving many of our brave comrades cut down by leaden messengers of death. As we reached the north bank of the stream, followed by the wildly cheering rebels, whose bullets came pattering the water like a first-class hail storm, the mass of rebels emerged from the timber into open land. The opportune moment had come for "Rosy" to spring his well laid trap. On the rocky bluff above us a long mass of cedars, which to a casual observer appeared a natural growth, suddenly became prostrate. Simultaneously the terrific discharge of sixty pieces of artillery, well charged with grape and canister, went crashing over our heads, plowing gaps of death and destruction in the heavy columns of the enemy. This threw them into disorder. General Jeff. C. Davis' division, and the greater part of Negley's division, rushed forward to the bank of the stream. Meanwhile, the scattered members of our brigade fell into line wherever opportunity afforded the best chance to return the enemy's fire. A desperate close range fight ensued. Our artillery continued to pour a deadly fire over our heads, and before the water ceased to squirt from our boot-legs the greater part of our command that remained alive and not dangerously wounded, re-entered the river, this time the pursuers. The enemy made a desperate and confused resistance, and at first were forced to gradually fall back, but soon were fleeing in a perfect rout. They continued this until they had reached the timber near Little's Creek. A dozen men, of Companies D and H, of the Eighth, were the first to straddle one piece of the noted Washington Battery, taken here from the enemy. Among them were Coe Howard, H. Harris and Samuel Everman, Company E. A few brave rebels were trying to drag off the piece, having thrown down their arms for that purpose, and the boys succeeded in capturing three of them, also. About this time, darkness put a stop to the bloody day's work. The spirit of Bragg's army was broken. As one of the half drunken prisoners expressed it. "We are whooped, fur our rations and whisky 's about out."

But we had suffered terribly. Every officer of the Eighth engaged in this battle was either wounded or killed, except four, Major Broadhus, Lieutenants Blackwell, Phips and myself. All of us had bullet holes in our clothing. The greater part of the uninjured of our boys spent the first half of the night on the field among the dead, dying and wounded of both armies, thickly strewn over the field and woodland pasture, in many places half a dozen men on a square rod of surface. We built up fires, and carried our bleeding comrades to them, and loaded them into ambulances as fast as we could procure them. Major Broadhus, of the Eighth, was indefatigable in procuring conveyances for our wounded comrades, riding from hospital to hospital, urging up the tired, sleepy ambulance drivers. Captain Banton had fallen on the picket line. Captains Minter and Hickman and Lieutenant W. B. Cox were mortally wounded. The other wounded who did not fall into the enemy's hands as prisoners, whose names will appear hereafter, were Lieutenant Colonel R. May, Lieutenant Wm. Park, Company C; Lieutenant Burley, Company G; Captain H. Thomas, Company K; Sergeant D. C. Winbourn, and thirty-seven other non-commissioned officers and privates of the Eighth were found and carried to farm houses in the vicinity of the battle ground.

Among the dead on the field, were Sergeant Baker, Company I; Moses Dunaway, Company D; B. McGuire, Company D; George Keaton, Company E; Jasper Collins, Company B; John Dearbin, Company D; Henry Sheppard, Company C; Chas.

Moore, Company B, and several others died of their wounds the next day. Our total loss was, five days after, reported to be seventy-nine killed and wounded, out of less than 300.

A short account of my own experience on this bloody field on that night will probably assist the reader to form a more correct idea of men, and their feelings and actions immediately after such a sanguinary engagement.

We turn from the fleeing enemy, flushed with victory, though purchased at, oh! what a price. We gave three cheers, and return to the timber, with those fluctuating emotions of exultation, mixed with pity, that often stirs the heart of the soldier. The deadly conflict is over, the fierce bloodthirsty lion of our nature gives way to the better and finer promptings of the human heart. As we tenderly lift the bleeding, mangled forms of our unfortunate comrades, four of us to a body, and carry them into prostrate groups around the fires, made to warm alike friends and now helpless foes. Our work of mercy goes on, and ambulance after ambulance is loaded with wounded. The cries and groans of familiar voices cause the rough, rude appearing soldiers' hearts to soften, and they become as sympathetic as our sisters and mothers. The surgeon had just finished probing and bandaging a mortal wound, and we were urging him to try and do something for the five ominous holes in the body of our brave, and now lamented messmate, Lieutenant Cox, who, with a score of others, was lying in a circle around the fire, on coats and blankets, the flickering fire causing their pale faces to wear a ghastly or unearthly appearance. Many of them were pronounced too far gone to be moved. While the surgeon was attending to his squad, myself and two others, of Company H, made a search for a stretcher, most of them now being at the various houses containing our suffering brethren, which a stream of armless and legless humanity were fast filling up. We went stumbling over the dead, now almost the sole occupants of the field. A man in a sitting position attracted our attention. We went to him, and tightened the bloody handkerchief around his thigh, that had a wound partly severing the main artery of that limb. He wore the uniform of a rebel lieutenant, and said he was from Woodford County, Kentucky. He asked us our State, and, upon being informed, took from his pocket a well worn miniature case, and requested me to send it to Miss M. Nickerson, Versailles, Kentucky. After a long hunt the stretcher was found, and at 3 o'clock a. m. of the 3d, during a hard rain, H. Harris, C. Howard, a soldier of the Fifty-first Ohio and myself, toiled over the slippery path, bearing upon our shoulders the body of our uncomplaining, but suffering comrade, Lieutenant Cox. On our arrival at the house we soon became very sick, the sight and smell of so much human blood, together with the fatigue and our long fast, causing us to leave the shelter and seek out a few comrades, on the river bank, around a struggling fire, where we got a cup of hot coffee. At that time Major Broadhus rode up, having just left the field, saying: "Lieutenant, I am about as near dead as any man with a whole skin in the army." He drank a cup of coffee, and, with a good blanket over us, we were soon asleep by a log, on a pile of drifted leaves, and for two hours forgot there had been a great battle, or that the rain was pouring down and soaking our leafy bed and clothing.

At 6 o'clock a. m. the rattle of drums aroused the slumbering troops. Wringing out some of our clothing, and taking some more of the black but invigorating coffee, our squad, accompanied by the major, struck out to find the remnant of our brigade. In retracing a part of the battle ground we found our rebel lieutenant still in death, having doubtless bled to death. During the day the Third Brigade collected and bivouacked on the north bank of the river. On account of the incessant rain, and having so much hospital work to do, nothing more than picket firing toward Murfreesboro occurred. During a heavy thunder storm, on the night of the 3d, the enemy made a feigned attack upon the center of our army. A short, but severe, skirmish ensued, causing us to arouse suddenly from our cozy beds of weeds and corn stalks, and stand in line two hours. We were not very anxious for a renewal of the fight, and, as the firing ceased, were not displeased to resume our peaceful if not luxurious couches. We remained here in the mud and water, with very little to eat, until the 7th, furnishing details to bury the dead of both armies, the enemy having made safe their retreat to Tullahoma. The inclement weather had delayed the unpleasant work. Our own dead were cared for first, and buried in single graves. But this mode was abandoned as too tedious, and several of the rebel dead were made to occupy one ditch, their "last." Company H's old Irishman, Tom, being among the fatigue party, was engaged in placing the bodies in the common grave. Some of his co-laborers remonstrated with Tom for tramping on the dead with his feet in order to straighten out their rigid limbs. This rough son of the "Emerald Isle" straightened up and cast a look of contempt at his more feeling comrades and said: "Hot, tot, mon! and what did ye's come down here for, then, if it weren't to put down the ribbils? Faith, an' it's more uv thim traithors I'd loik to be puttin' down this same way. May the saints save us, but indade I would. Now, b'ys, hand me in that long yeller-haired one nixt," and the solemn work proceeded.

CHAPTER IX.

The rebels evacuated Murfreesboro and their snug winter quarters during the hard rain on the night of the 3d January, and many of the inhabitants also fled from their comfortable homes, taking their slaves with them.

On the morning of the 7th, the Third Brigade marched from their muddy bivouack on the river bank, and crossed the river on the remains of the railroad bridge. We passed through the once pretty, neat county seat of Rutherford county. Its war-worn and torn, tumble-down appearance, caused some of us to feel sad. All public and many private buildings were full of wounded of both armies. Surgeons, wearing both the blue and grey, could be seen hurrying to and fro on the streets. Cavalry horses and ambulance mules were hitched to ornamental and shade trees, the nice fencing having disappeared from many fine suburban residences. Our command halted one mile from town on the Lebanon Pike, and were making preparations for supper, when we were hurried out on picket, Major Broadhus commanding the Eighth, and were until after dark establishing the lines, with about one-third of the command on duty and the remainder in reserve. Rations were scarce, large quantities of government stores having been destroyed during the battle by rebel cavalry, and the L. & N. Railroad yet unrepaired, caused us to economize the half rations we were then subsisting on. Some of the Eighth boys, during the night, were lucky enough to knock over a fat porker, which added materially to the weight of our lank haversacks and stomachs.

On returning to where the brigade was on the 8th, we were as much pleased as surprised to again see our old, leaky Sibley tents and cooking utensils. We had felt the need of these useful, almost indispensable articles for over two weeks. The brigade quartermaster also replaced the boys' blankets and overcoats they had so readily and willingly parted with after the battle, that the wounded might have the benefit of them.

The 9th, myself and several others of the Eighth went into town to look up wounded friends. In an old vacated store house we found James Moreland and John Wilson, of Company H, John Wise and about half a dozen other boys, all of whom got over their wounds except Wilson, who, though dangerously wounded, gave a weak little cheer as we entered. In another house we found private Waters, Company C, in the same room with one of his brothers, wearing the grey rebel uniform, who also had a serious wound, having received it while in the rebel ranks in our front on the 2d.

On the 10th, I procured a pass and the loan of Major Broadhus' horse, and rode back across the river to the field hospital, where Captain Hickman, Lieutenant Cox and the principal part of our wounded were. H. English and Wm. Herndon, Company B, each had lost a foot; Ike Thomas, Company H, a leg; Sergeant Winbourn had a hole through his chest; and in the next room lay the above named officers, evidently within a few hours of death. They recognized and talked to me. Captain Winbourn had arrived from Nashville, and, being yet feeble in health, was performing the self-imposed task of remaining with his two dying comrades. Captain Minter had died the day previous, and the other two officers above named gave up their young, cheerful and promising lives the following day. Their remains were sent home to be buried by kind friends and relatives.

The morning of the 13th we moved camp into a piece of timber midway between the Nashville and Lebanon Pikes and one and a half miles north of town. Major Broadhus appointed a board of officers to survey and condemn our old tents. We received new ones of the Bell pattern, and men and officers generally turned out to brick masonry, erecting chimneys from the same materials the rebels had used for a like purpose. In a few days we were well quartered and drawing full rations once more.

The 18th, Colonel Barnes returned, and the following day Lieutenant Smallwood arrived with a few absentees, whom Morgan's raid had prevented from joining us before the battle.

As soon as we began to get comfortably settled in our new tents, orders for heavy details began to pour in from headquarters for pickets, fatigue and forage duty. A large part of the command worked daily on fortifications. Some days the regiment would guard a long line of empty wagons into the country, and collect corn, oats, fodder or corn blades. On these expeditions the Eighth boys never forgot that men had to be fed as well as army mules, and many little creature comforts were brought in to season and vary our regular rations. The 25th our regiment escorted a train out five miles toward Lebanon, and returned with heavy loads of corn. Again, the 27th, the Eighth and Thirty-fifth Indiana, under Major Broadhus, with fifty teams, proceeded through and three miles beyond the place we had been a few days before, and turned into the plantation owned by a portly old rebel named Atkins. He had a great quantity of corn, and when he saw how many wagons we had, and with what speed the soldiers, with the help of his willing, grinning " niggers," could lower his well filled cedar log cribs, he indulged in considerable profanity, until Major Broadhus informed him that he should have a government voucher for his produce. After having explained to him what "voucher" meant, and seeing that his blowing threats were not heeded, the old fellow cooled down a little. Meantime some of the boys were trying to persuade the no less portly and equally indignant landlady to sell them a few chickens. Being refused in not over mild language, some of the Thirty-fifth undertook to help themselves. The major then ordered the writer to take a guard of five men and protect the house and poultry. By this duty I soon assumed the role of especial protector and friend, and succeeded in purchasing from her two nice bacon hams. After weighing them, she "'lowed they'd fetch four dollars." I handed her a V greenback. She scornfully refused the legal tender, saying, "I won't have nothin' to do with you'ens shinplasters." Then she smilingly gave me change for a confederate "blueback." By this time, the train being loaded and in motion, Major Broadhus and the puffing old southerner came in to fill out his voucher. This done, he set out his bottle of "old peach and sugar." After we had tasted and praised his liquor, and were about to leave, the now genial old fellow said: "Well, me nor the old 'oman nuther kin read, and the gals is off; you jest read that ar voucher fur me." When the major came to the closing sentence, i. e., "to be paid on proof of loyalty," a sudden change came over our hospitable friend; his anger and profanity were fearful. As we reached the yard fence we heard him say: "By h—ll! ef it depends on that, I know I'll never get a cent." We did not tarry to discuss the probabilities of the case. Some of the teams "stalled," as the drivers call it, delaying us so much it was very late when we arrived in camp.

The 30th, the entire regiment able for duty worked on fortifications. About this time our absent officers returned, and with them came the remainder of our absentees able for duty, a few of them having been absent without leave since November. All these except one were restored to their proper standing, with loss of pay while absent. The exception was private

"Scabber," who, through the influence of some bad men, enemies to the government, had shunned and tried to evade the officer, to whom he should have reported, and consequently he had to face a general court martial.

February 1st, at dark, the regiment had orders to be ready at 6 o'clock the next morning to escort another forage train. The bugleman overslept himself, and we just had fifteen minutes to prepare and eat our breakfast. The reader will understand that military orders, like time and tide, wait for no man. Many of us, therefore, ate our hard tack and drank our tin of coffee marching along the Lebanon Pike. This time we went eleven miles before we began to load our wagons. A heavy rain retarded our work. As there were some indications of attack by rebel cavalry, the Eighth formed the rear guard and the Fifty-first Ohio the advance on the return. We saw no armed enemies that day, and arrived in camp near midnight, tired and ravenously hungry.

The 3d day of February there were several promotions in our line to fill vacancies occasioned by death. Several of these commissions from the governor of Kentucky bore the following clause: " Promoted for gallant and meritorious conduct at the battle of Stone River."

The 10th, the news of the action of Congress, authorizing the employment of "contrabands" as teamsters, laborers and cooks, in the United States service, also that a bill was before congress for the arming and equipping of a certain number of negro troops, was received, and became the one great theme of discussion with the soldiers, especially in Kentucky regiments. A few of our officers and quite a number of the men appeared to still favor the idea of putting down the rebellion without seriously molesting the "divine institution" of slavery, some contending it foolish, as the "nigger wouldn't fight, nohow," while others, with indignation, declared that every white soldier would be disgraced by fighting in the ranks along with the colored troops. Two or three officers became so jealous of their "honor, sir," they privately talked of resigning. But a very large majority of the Eighth, rank and file, contended that it was plainly the duty of the government to empower our generals to "use all and every available means to suppress or put down this wicked and useless rebellion." Captain Smallwood and several other officers immediately took a firm stand favoring the measure, and in a discussion between the former and one of his company, who had become very boisterous about "nigger equality," the captain said, in the hearing of his company, "Boys, when we entered the service we each took a solemn oath that we would obey the orders of the president of the United States and other superior officers. We then were desperately in earnest, and meant just what we said, and I have no reason to wish to violate that pledge, and by the help of God I intend to keep it to the very best of my ability. Nor do I yet believe that any of you who have done and suffered so much are willing to see this grand old republic split up into contemptible little provinces, always fighting to destroy each other. No, boys, we must maintain our nationality, whatever becomes of slavery. I know, and you all know, that the southern slave-holders have themselves given the first mortal wound to slavery. Now we say, let the accursed, barbarous, traitor-breeding institution die. Let no true soldier try to staunch its wound, or care that the consequences of this war gives the poor slave his freedom." Continuing on the subject, he said: "Boys, havn't you learned that Buell's policy of trying to whip the rebels with a part of our forces and protecting their property with the other part, guarding cornfields and chicken roosts for rich rebels, will no longer do? I say no! Let the fettered slave loose; let him flee to our camps to cook; drive mules, dig earthworks; and if congress and the president see proper to arm them to help crush the rebellion, we should not object. No, I would not object, if it were possible and practicable, to arm a regiment of mules or jackasses and let them charge the enemy; and, I conclude, if Cuffee is to have his freedom, he should be allowed to place his carcass where it may save the lives of many good white men. Now, Company K, you have my opinion. You all have an equal right to yours, but I shall do my duty, and expect you all to do the same." Before the close of the war nearly every man of the Eighth began to look at the negro question like the captain.

During the month of February a good many of our wounded boys died; among them George English, Company B; I. Thomas and John Wilson, Company H. Also, Lieutenant Newton Hughes and Sergeant Combs, Company I, and private Richardson, Company H., died from disease contracted by exposure. I attended a few of these burials.

The bodies of Hughes, Richardson and Combs were put into rough coffins, which a few of our men constructed out of rough boards taken from a vacant dwelling. It was the best we could do under the circumstances, and much better than the majority of our dead could be treated. We felt our need of a chaplain in this sad duty. But a few remarks and a short prayer, then we laid them away, placing cedar slabs with name, company and regiment, cut in plain letters, at the head of each. The last few days of February the company commanders were very busy preparing pay rolls.

On the evening of the 3d of March, the Eighth and Fifty-first Ohio had orders to prepare to march early next morning, consequently preparations were made, and at 7 o'clock a. m. all the Eighth, except a few sick, were marching on the Lebanon pike, commanded by Major Broadhus, Colonel Barnes being again called to Kentucky on official business. We halted at the ford of Stone River and pitched our camp on the south side, for the purpose of remaining here to guard a pontoon bridge, that the rebel cavalry had tried twice to destroy. By dark we were tolerably well quartered, but felt sadly the loss of our good fire places and chimneys, it being cold and damp weather, and expecting to remain here some time. The 5th we demolished a large brick smith shop, and at night the majority of us were enjoying the cheerful warmth of fires in our rudely constructed chimneys.

The morning of the 9th we were ordered to return to Murfreesboro. On our return the men appeared much pleased at the idea of again occupying their original encampment. When opposite that place our wagons, containing camp and garrison equipage, halted, and we were joined by the balance of the brigade, with orders to make reconnoissance or demonstration against the enemy's picket, on the Shelbyville road. Five miles south of town we passed our outer pickets, and two miles further came in sight of their mounted videttes. The brigade formed in line of battle, with a strong line of skirmishers in advance. We pressed forward a mile further, the enemy only exchanging a few shots with our skirmish line, and then fell back to Hoover's Gap. We bivouacked in line of battle among the dense growth of cedars, with orders to keep forward a strong line of pickets, and wait the enemy's attack. About midnight our cavalry videttes and the rebels' advance commenced a lively popping of pistols and carbines. The darkness prevented any serious harm. Soon after, the rain began to descend, and continued to fall all day, the 10th, on our unprotected bodies. In the afternoon of that day the rain increased into a miniature flood. This appeared to keep the Johnnies in our front quite peacable, and as we had no orders to advance, we felt satisfied to hover over our smoking cedar rails, more to protect the rain from extinguishing our fires than to derive any comforting warmth therefrom, and to add to our unpleasant situation, our rations were out, or rather, had been left in the wagons on leaving Stone River, the previous day. At last, as the gloomy darkness of this miserable day began to settle over the earth, we gladly received the order to form the brigade with as little noise as possible, after which we halted on the pike in column, where we were forced to stand in the cold mud and water for two hours, waiting for two companies of the Twenty-first Kentucky, who had been placed out on picket during the day, in the thick cedars. The night being very dark, and no loud talking permitted, the adjutant and brigade picket officer had much difficulty in finding them. The welcome command, "forward," was at last given, and we soon measured off the seven miles to Murfreesboro. As we marched through that quiet city our boys struck up this song:

> "Sometimes we have to double-quick;
> This Dixie mud is mighty slick.
> The soldier's fare is very rough,
> The bread is hard, and beef is tough,
> That's the way they put us through,
> I tell you what, it's hard to do.
> But we'll obey duty's call,
> To conquer Dixie, that is all!"

We entered our old encampment, north of Murfreesboro, at midnight, and were much pleased to find the wagoners and convalescents had all our tents up for us.

The 12th of March, 1863, Major Johnson paid the Eighth Kentucky four months' pay. Full pockets generally caused smiling faces; but many of the boys were in debt to the sutler, while others had wives and families at home that needed, and generally received, all the husband could spare. Soon the majority of our men only had left a little "tobacco money."

The 13th General VanCleve, "grandpap," as the boys called him, returned, healed of his wound, and again took command of the Third Division.

The 18th the Twenty-first Army Corps was reviewed by General Rosecrans. The next day we moved our camp a half mile further north, in the edge of a cotton field, near Little's Creek, where the other regiments of the Third Brigade were already encamped.

The 22d Colonel Barnes returned from Kentucky and took command of the brigade, Colonel Matthews being absent on leave of absence. The same day Captain Winbourn, Company H, and Captain Jamison, Company D, resigned on account of ill health, and returned home. Here all the brigade decorated our well arranged encampment with long avenues of cedar trees, planted to shade and beautify our white tented village.

The latter part of March we began daily drills. Our stylish, vigilant (and as some of our boys thought, over particular), brigade inspector, Captain Woods, of the Fifty-first Ohio, having reported some of the Eighth boys for a trivial omission, invoked the displeasure of the whole command. From some cause, one morning, the inspector made his morning trip around our pickets rather earlier than usual, and was galloping along near the bank of Little's Creek, where the thick timber and dense fog in the early dawn made objects at a short distance very indistinct, when, from the opposite side of the muddy stream, came in unmistakable distinctness to the captain's ears:

"Halt! who comes there?"

He replied, "brigade inspector."

Sentinel—"I know no man in the dark. Dismount, advance, and give the countersign."

The captain looked at the miry, filthy stream, and began to parley with the obdurate sentinel.

The repetition of the word "advance," accompanied by the ominous click of the gun lock, settled the matter instantly. With hands raised, his polished boots and gold-corded pants reeking with muddy water, that official leaned over the point of Campbell's bayonet, and spoke the password: "You are too soon, captain."

April 1st we had orders to draw and cook five days' rations, each man with 100 rounds, and be ready to march at sunrise, the 2d. Accordingly, our brigade, now under Colonel Matthews, a battery of light artillery and two regiments of cavalry, all under the command of General Stanley, marched early out the Liberty road. The day was warm for the season, the long rest had refreshed our men, and we tripped along after the cavalry lively, but before night many of the men became much wearied. We bivouacked twenty miles from Murfreesboro, near a village called Auburn. At midnight the troops were all awakened without bugle or drum, and in comparative silence resumed the march toward Liberty, where we expected to find about 5,000 mounted rebels, under Robert Breckinridge. About sunrise we waded Smith's fork of Duck River, halted and ate our breakfast. Here we were joined by some East Tennessee cavalry. At 11 o'clock we passed through Liberty, and hurried on up Dry Creek, and found the Johnnies occupying the mount on the south, called Snow Hill. The brigade formed line with two companies from each regiment thrown forward as skirmishers, and the cavalry sent round to flank the enemy, with orders to gain their rear. With quick-step we ascended the steep, rocky mountain. When near the summit the enemy's pickets opened a scattering fire on us, that went harmlessly over our heads. Our advance charged on them before they could reload. They fled down the opposite slope to their second line of dismounted cavalry, who lay protected by a rude breastwork of logs and stone. We engaged them in a short skirmish. By this time our artillery had got in position and began to shell the Johnnies. General Stanley, who, like all the other staff officers, was on foot, walked down among our boys, and asked, "What regiment is this?"

"The Eighth Kentucky, was the response.

"Well, Kentuckians are not afraid! charge on them rascals, and shoot their heads off."

With a yell, our skirmishers, Companies A and B, and a score of volunteers from other companies, pitched forward at a double-quick. The rebels fled to where their horses were, over another hill, leaving several dead and six prisoners in our hands. The cavalry now attacked, and ran the enemy off toward Smithville. Our loss was only three wounded. This ended our Snow Hill battle.

Our infantry force returned to Liberty, where we bivouacked for the night.

The 4th we started on our return, and reached Alexandria, county seat of DeKalb County, ten miles west of Liberty. We awaited the return of the cavalry, and near night moved seven miles toward Lebanon.

The 5th, early in the morning, we resumed the march through Cherry Valley, a beautiful farming district. At Sharp's Springs, a small village, we found a store containing a considerable quantity of Confederate stores. We had no transportation to remove them, and before all the force had passed the store "took fire." We then passed through Lebanon and bivouacked seven miles from that place. Our peaceful sleep was interrupted twice during the night by the reports of our cavalry's carbines. They brought in three prisoners the next morning, said to have been bushwhackers. We arrived at our old camp, near Murfreeboro, on the 6th.

We resumed our usual routine of daily duty, to wit: Reveille, at 5 a. m.

First—Regiments form on their respective parade grounds, and stand to arms one hour.

Second—Breakfast at 7 o'clock.

Third—Guard mounting, at 8 o'clock, of thirty-five men and two officers for picket, ten men and one officer for camp guard.

Fourth—Company drill from 9 to 11 o'clock.

Fifth—Dinner.

Sixth—Battalion and brigade drill from 2 to 4 p. m.

Seventh—Dress parade at 5, supper at 6, and tattoo at 8 o'clock p. m.

Thus life again begun with us. So constantly was every soldier employed, that one day each week was allowed for "wash day." Washing with us was as much of a duty as fighting. Woe unto the unlucky sloven that appeared at Sunday morning inspection with dirty clothes, dirty hands, long hair or untrimmed beard. Wash day with the Eighth boys brought its amusements, as well as its vexations. The latter grew less with us as we became thoroughly initiated into the mysteries of washing, rinsing and wringing, and some fastidious boys would worry over an imperfect or badly washed shirt as much as their mothers or sisters ever did over their soiled linen.

In the House of Representatives of the State of Kentucky, March 2d, 1863, Messrs. Cleveland and Burnham were appointed a committee on the part of the House to receive from the Governor certain flags of Kentucky troops. At the appointed hour the Senate repaired to the House for the purpose indicated in a former resolution. At noon Mr. Wickliff, Secretary of State, appeared with the storm-tossed and war worn flags of the Fifteenth, Seventeenth, Sixth, Ninth, Eighth and Twenty-first Regiments of Kentucky volunteer infantry, together with a message from the governor, giving a short history of each flag. In that message, in referring to the flags of the Eighth and Twenty-first, he said:

"These mementoes, which I have the honor to place at your disposal, were brought from Tennessee. They are storm-tossed and leaden-tattered flags presented to me for preservation, along with other mementoes of the terrible realities of the existing convulsion. Under these riddled colors many cherished sons of Kentucky have met death in this cruel and unnatural war. We are pleased to have been the bearer to this body of these flags, that were borne amid the storm of battle by our gallant sons. It will be observed that the colors of the Eighth Regiment (Colonel Barnes) is almost completely destroyed. It was upheld, amid showers of shot and shell, by Edgar Park, Company C, until the missiles of the foe had pierced again and again its every fold. Finally, the staff was struck and shivered to pieces. The enemy was crowding closely around the undaunted standard-bearer. The broken staff could no longer be grasped, but he quickly gathered the remnants of the flag and bore them rapidly to those who so nobly defended it, with an intrepidity rarely equaled and never surpassed. These standards, around which cluster so many glorious memories, it is hoped, will be placed in the archives of the State, while others will be furnished to take their places in the field."

CHAPTER X.

The 10th of April our encampment was aroused by the report of rebel guerrillas capturing a train near Lavergne, and robbing the passengers of money and other valuables, our jolly musician, P. D. Schull, being among the unfortunate victims.

As the weather grew warmer our battalion and brigade evening drills became less enjoyable. All the survivors will long remember the amount of toil and sweat these knapsack drills cost them on that old cotton field. On this same old field, the 13th, the brigade formed. The men had all blacked their shoes, and donned their best appearance, and the officers were in dress parade outfit. We passed in review of General VanCleve ("Grand-pap"), who had just returned, with his wound healed. The command then formed square by divisions, closed in mass. Into the center rode Colonel Matthews, seated on his noted yellow horse, and accompanied by his staff. He made us his farewell address, having been elected mayor of Cincinnati, Ohio. He had endeared himself to every regiment, and many regretted his having to leave us, though the Eighth boys felt some pride at Colonel Barnes taking his place as commander of the brigade; and as Lieutenant Colonel May had been promoted to colonel of the Seventh Kentucky, Major Broadhus thus took command of the Eighth, but his failing health and emaciated looks convinced many of us that we would soon lose him too.

The 20th April our pleasant faced old paymaster again paid us a visit and our allowance of greenbacks for January and February. The last company had received pay by 9 o'clock, p. m., and many had retired to bed, when we were ordered to march immediately toward Lebanon. The enemy was reported to be advancing. Our new rolls of greenbacks were hastily left with a few convalescents, fearing the fortunes of war might place them in the hands of rebels, who were anxious to get some of "you'ens money." With a fresh supply of cartridges and rations, the brigade hurried out past the pickets, who were now on the *qui vive*. Our blood was up, and a cheerful inclination for fight pervaded the ranks. This sanguinary feeling increased when we came in hearing of a clattering noise in advance of us, supposed to be rebel cavalry on the hard stone road. We hurried from column into line, and, with fixed bayonets, awaited the expected charge of the mounted enemy. A few cavalry videttes of ours returned and reported to Colonel Barnes that the supposed enemy was about a hundred negroes at a vacant house in front of us holding a mammoth jubilee, and their vigorous dancing was so spirited and executed with so much vim that our pickets mistook the sound for advancing foes. Our men received this explanation with loud cheers, and returned to camp, leaving the innocent but noisy darkies enjoying themselves over their newly-found freedom.

April 27th, Major Broadhus resigned. The line officers met and passed resolutions expressing their high esteem for the major. His bravery and cheerful company had made him the lasting friend of all of the command, and general regret was felt at the loss of his company. The next day the writer was present when Lieutenant Carson presented the major with a copy of the resolutions. He appeared much affected, and expressed his thanks, through an officer, to the regiment, saying his love for all and sorrow at parting admonished him to avoid a public leave-taking. Regret was depicted on every face as he silently took each man by the hand to say farewell.

Again, the evening of the 8th of May, we were made sad to part with another one of our good officers. Lieutenant Colonel Reuben May, having recovered from his wound received at Stone River, had returned to the regiment only for the purpose of arranging a few small private affairs and bid us farewell, having been promoted to colonel of the Seventh Kentucky Infantry, for gallant and meritorious conduct on the battlefield of Stone River. That evening, at dress parade, he made us his farewell address. I can give only an extract of his appropriate little speech: "Boys, we have made many hard marches together. We have met the enemy more than once, and have always driven them. This regiment has the name of being the bravest of the brave, and I have been promoted for my gallantry and bravery, but I do not deserve it. It is you boys who have won for me that honor. I shall ever remember and honor every one of you." At the conclusion of the lieutenant colonel's remarks, Major Clark proposed three cheers for Colonel May. They were given with a will, but the writer noticed many of the men's voices quivered with emotion.

The 12th May, Lieutenant Colonel Mayhew and Major Clark were "married" to their late commissions, having recently been promoted. As custom required, every officer, when promoted, was expected to give his brother officers in the regiment a wedding supper, and this double wedding, at Keneday's sutler tent, will long be remembered by the survivors of the old Eighth.

In our cheerfulness and banqueting over our recently promoted officers, we did not forget our fallen brave comrades, whose decaying bodies lay within one mile of camp, in their rude bare graves. On Sunday morning, the 17th of May, a squad of officers and men, being provided with a picket pass, and a well lettered cedar board for each one of the dead of the Eighth (bearing the name, rank, company and regiment), and a spade, proceeded to that part of the battlefield where, on the 2d of January, 1863, Breckenridge's half-drunken rebels fought our brigade. After a long search among the thousands of unmarked or indifferently marked graves, we found the particular ones sought for. Placing the proper boards well into the earth, the graves were refilled, and a nice mound made over the once brave and cheerful comrade. After paying this last tender tribute to our dead, we took a walk over this memorable field and woodland, now converted into a vast graveyard. We noticed in many trees not larger than a man's body as many as sixty musket ball holes, and great numbers of trees were shivered and torn to splinters by solid shot. The tiny, delicate flowers, springing fresh from this blood-enriched soil, reminded us of how much, indeed, like the flower or grass are we poor mortals—some, like the aged man, grow to full maturity, and the hoar frosts of winter cause them to wither and die; while others, like those we plucked so fresh, reminded us of our youthful, heroic dead comrades, cut off in the full bloom and vigor of life, both by the index finger of man's hand. The bad odor from many of the shallow graves rendered our stay much shorter than it would otherwise have been.

About this time Surgeon Morton was assigned to our command.

The 1st of May the officers of the Eighth organized themselves into a class for the study of Casey's Tactics. One hour each day was spent in "school" recitations, but the various duties of the officers seriously interfered with regular attendance. In about three weeks our studies were, as before, principally confined to private study.

The 25th of May our men were much pleased at being ordered to turn in the old Springfield muskets and receive therefor the Enfield rifles, the arms they had long been desiring. Two days later we thought we would soon get to try their efficiency at flesh and blood, as General Rosecrans issued an order for all the troops to have five days' rations constantly on hand, especially as "Captain" Bragg's forces began to show hostile demonstrations about Wartrace and Hoover's Gap.

During our long stay here we had many reviews and inspections by brigade inspectors, beside our regular Sunday morning company inspection. The third week in May we had no less than three of these, as the boys called them, "troublesome parades," where knapsacks were packed and repacked, the entire contents of the soldiers' scant wardrobe, to the smallest article, viewed and reviewed. Some of the men, having overdrawn regulation value of clothing the first year, now began to economize, and many could not parade more than one well worn clean shirt. After the regular Sunday inspection, the first Sunday in May, Sergeant Wood presented himself at my tent and inquired if there would be any issue of clothing soon. He was asked why. "Well, Cap'n, that old shirt of mine has been viewed so often lately, and old Captain Wood looked so infernal contemptuous the other day when he asked me if that was all the underwear I had, and you were good enough not to say anything this morning, I want to get a new shirt, just to please my namesake, as inspections appear to be increasing. One fellow in Company A got thunder from the division inspector, the other day, just because he had only one pair of socks in his knapsack. Set me down, captain, 'underwear.'" About this time Lieutenant Colonel Mayhew ordered that the man who could show the cleanest gun and equipage at weekly inspection should have a free pass for one week within the picket lines. There was much interest manifested and much labor expended in polishing arms. At dress parade, the 13th, the adjutant read the lieutenant colonel's order, "That Corporal Wm. Smith, Company D, be excused from all duty and have a free pass for five days." This increased the number of aspirants for the brightest gun, and gave rise to an amusing incident in Company H. "Dobin Spikes," noted for spending the least time and labor on washing clothes and rubbing his gun, now became equally interested in the various materials used in polishing guns. At supper he said: "Gosh, boys, what does Conner and Smith and these other fellers put on their guns to keep 'em bright?" One of his comrades, with much secresy, informed him that it was nothing else but "bean juice." At the expense of his stomach, "Dobin" gave his musket a good coat, and, as the inside was not the brightest, he also filled it up and set it away for the night. Early next morning the orderly notified "Dobin" to get ready for picket. In his hurry about breakfast he gathered his gun, hastily rubbed off the thick mixture of dissolved beans, grease and salt, and forgot all about the contents of the barrel, until in line, and the adjutant gave the command, "Spring rammers!" "Dobin," in his great dilemma, exclaimed: "Good God! mine's full of bean soup!" "Dobin Spikes" was ordered to be put on extra duty for appearing at guard mounting with his gun unserviceable, and spent the greater part of the day extracting bean soup from the rusty bore of his prize gun.

The 1st day of June, First Lieutenant Gumm, Company D, Lieutenant Ketchins, Company A, Lieutenant Smallwood, Company K, Lieutenant Martin, Company I, and Lieutenant Wright, Company H, all received commissions as captains of their respective companies, Captains Jamison, Thomas, McDaniel and Winbourn having resigned, and Captain Mayhew having been promoted to the position of lieutenant colonel. The second lieutenants and first sergeants of those companies also received promotions at the same time, to fill vacancies occasioned by these new captains. The marriage supper at our sutler's on this occasion was a lively and expensive, if not an extensive affair. The majority of the Twenty-first Kentucky officers were present.

The 16th June, General VanCleve's division, including the Eighth, formed into three sides of a hollow square, and witnessed the execution of a deserter from the Ninth Kentucky, named Minx. It was a sad and shocking scene, causing a soldier to feel different from witnessing a true, brave comrade falling in battle. This was the first, and, I am proud to say, the last military execution we witnessed.

The 18th, the division was reviewed by General Rosecrans. The same day Colonel Barnes put our brigade through a two hours' knapsack drill—not a pleasant recreation in hot weather, at least that was the general verdict of the Eighth boys.

The sentence of the court martial that tried "Scabber" was read by Adjutant Park, on dress parade, the 18th, which was, "To wear a ball and chain in and about the camp of the Eighth Regiment Kentucky Volunteer Infantry six months." The command generally felt the shame and disgrace that the good-natured, light-minded offender should have felt, and when the smith fastened on John's "jewelry," nearly every man sympathized to some degree with him as being made an example of.

At last, by great diligence and energy, General Rosecrans succeeded in bringing the Army of the Cumberland up to its best possible condition.

On the 23d June, our commander ordered a general forward movement of all the forces about Murfreesboro, except the Third (our) Division of Crittenden's corps. The rebel army occupied a strong position, extending from Shelbyville to Wartrace, about parallel with Duck River, with their base of supplies at Tullahoma. To follow up this victorious army in its respective movements, which resulted in forcing Bragg's army to flee to the south side of the Tennessee River, would increase this volume to greater size than contemplated; therefore, we will refer the reader to a general history of the war, and follow up the movements of our particular regiment and brigade. While our comrades in front were marching through the rain and mud to dislodge the enemy, our division struck tents and moved inside the earthworks, trying to make ourselves as comfortable as the circumstances would permit, believing, as our division general was an old man, that we had been left to garrison the place, and would probably remain here a considerable time. We sympathized with our comrades in front, whose guns we could hear thundering away at the enemy.

On the 29th we were rejoiced to see 500 rebel prisoners brought back, captured at Shelbyville, where General Stanley's troops had rescued from sentence of death our brave and daring female spy, Miss Major Cushman.

The 30th day of June the Third Brigade, under command of Colonel Barnes, received orders to march immediately toward McMinnville, with no baggage except shelter tents and blankets; all tents and officers' desks to be left in care of the convalescents of each regiment. At that time all the wagons and teams were in constant use dragging supplies through the mud and rain to the front. At 4 o'clock p. m. we formed column and moved out on the Woodbury Pike. The continued rains had made the much used roads very muddy. A march of ten miles brought us to Cripple Creek, where we bivouacked.

July 1st was one of those still, clear, hot days, that usually succeeds a heavy rain in that climate. The power of the sun on the steaming earth and vegetation caused many of the boys to give out before noon. At that hour we arrived at Woodbury. Our shelter tents were soon pitched near this rebellious town, twenty miles from Murfreesboro. The next morning the Eighth, with a small squad of cavalry, made a scouting party, and went nine miles toward McMinnville, where Robert Breckinridge and a force of rebel cavalry were reported to be. The heat was oppressive, and quite a number of our men "fagged out," really overpowered with heat. The writer, being one of the number, will never forget the kindness of Major Clark, who, always ready to do an act of kindness to a comrade, placed me on his horse, while he footed it back to town. Our cavalry went quite near McMinnville, but found no sign of the enemy. I was told by Surgeon Robison that I had fever. He procured lodging for me in the house of a Mr. Burger, the only Union man of the town. His loyalty, and kindness to myself and Captain Millard, of the Twenty-first Kentucky, probably caused him the loss of his house and contents. We will give the reader this one incident of hundreds of similar cases of rebel hate and revenge. On entering the commodious dwelling, my feebleness caused an immediate introduction to a good bed—the first feathers I had reclined my weary limbs on for many months. I soon discovered that I had fallen into the hands of real Samaritans. Captain Millard and a few other sick occupied other rooms. There were also about twenty Union refugees, women and men, returning to their homes, yet inside the enemy's lines. The next day all our division arrived, bringing the good news of "Rosey's" recent victory over Bragg at Tullahoma. Mr. Burger's two daughters and some of the refugees gave vent to their joy by indulging in a few patriotic songs. Soon after one of the daughters of Burger came to my bed with a tempting morsel of supper for me. I asked: "Do many of your citizens rejoice with you over Union victories?" "No, indeed, captain; I greatly fear for papa when you all leave. I have seen some of them paying close attention to our house. They are indignant at us for sheltering you and those good Union people." About 8 o'clock everything became quiet except the heavy breathing of some weary sleeping refugees, and at last the extra dose of morphia caused me to drop into a troubled sleep. At length I awoke with a smothering, choking sensation. When first I struggled to consciousness smoke and flames were bursting into my room. I cried "fire!" as loud as my weakness permitted, and rolled out on to the floor, and gathered my clothing, haversack, sword and pistol from the chair into my arms. Unable to stand, I lay yelling "fire!" and kicking a snoring refugee, who suddenly sprang up, with half a dozen others. One heavy fellow rushing around the room in the blinding, hot smoke, hunting for the door, jumped on my chest, and I lost all consciousness until I felt myself being dragged through the dewy dog fennel in the yard. Some one had burst open the door just in time to save me from the horrid flames. All the inmates were in the yard, most of them destitute of raiment, except that in which they slept. I still had my effects (except my watch, which was lost,) clutched in my arms. The fine house and its valuable contents were entirely consumed, and from where the fire originated, it undoubtedly was a base act of incendiarism. Surgeon Robison and a soldier of the Eighth assisted me to a place near called "The Hotel," where I lay until daylight, a prey to the hungry bedbugs. As the ambulance, which contained myself and another sick man, drove out of town the next morning after our command, we passed an old smith shop, where Mr. Burger's family had taken refuge. I paid my bill and called for Miss Melissa, who had waited on me, and gave her ten dollars, and we left this sad, good man, almost penniless, but, as he said, yet loyal.

The division marched to within six miles of McMinnville, where the whole command arrived next day, the 7th of July, and formed an encampment half a mile east of town. While erecting shelter tents, a heavy rain was pouring down. I was fortunate enough to get quartered with a citizen of the town, where I remained ten days.

On our arrival at McMinnville the resident unionists appeared to be overjoyed at their deliverance from the "tender mercies" of John Morgan and his band, and to again see their friends return from their exile of eleven months.

The 10th of July we received the welcome news of the surrender of Vicksburg. About this time we had favorable reports from the Army of the Potomac. Our artillery was used freely in our rejoicings at the prospect of soon subduing the rebellion. Bright were many of our anticipations of an early return home to friends. But we knew not the many hard marches and bloody battles, death and starvation, that awaited many of us before final victory should crown our labors.

The 14th our wagon train arrived from Murfreesboro containing our regimental baggage.

The 18th the Eighth moved a few hundred yards, and were soon dwelling in a nicely shaded and decorated encampment, which was kept scrupulously clean during our stay here. Nearly every day heavy details from some brigade was sent out foraging, and the men usually returned with something "fresh" for their messmates.

The 18th I had recovered and reported for duty, and the next day took command of a foraging party of one hundred men and twenty wagons. I knew of a rich old rebel, living seven miles from camp, and, arriving there, we found a large field of oats ready for the sickle. The men went to work with a dozen old mowing scythes and traps of cradles, borrowed from farms along our road. It was cloudless and hot, but the thermometer did not stand as near the boiling point as did Mr. Snipe's temper, while his oaths and threats were treated as idle vaporings by his unbidden harvest hands. He received his voucher without comment, and, as the loaded wagons filed out into the road, the high-toned, indignant landlord discovered about a score of his chickens departing with the train. We left him trying to exhaust his vocabulary of denunciations against Yankees in general, and us in particular.

The 29th Major Johnston paid the regiment four

months' pay, and the 30th Orderly F. P. Wood left for Kentucky on furlough, carrying a considerable sum of money for the soldiers' wives and families living in Madison and Estill Counties.

The Eighth Regiment went on a foraging expedition the 4th of August. Two men failed to answer at roll call. Lieutenant Colonel Mayhew ordered them tied up by the thumbs. On our return to camp the order was obeyed, but with a strong protest from Captain Benton, in whose company the men belonged. Again, the 6th, a part of the regiment, on returning from a scout, when near town private Burgess, of Company H, in his persevering efforts to capture a fat hen, on which he had set his eyes and heart, failed to overtake the command before our arrival in camp, as he had promised me he would. Lieutenant Colonel Mayhew remained seated on his horse until the completion of roll call. When Burgess failed to answer, Lieutenant Colonel Mayhew said, "Captain Wright, I want you to tie that man up by the thumbs two hours, in the morning." I made no reply. After guard mounting, the following morning, the lieutenant colonel sent Adjutant Park with a message to me, requesting an interview at headquarters. I need not recite here, only that I politely, but firmly, refused to tie up Burgess, opposing the mode of punishment, especially for trivial offenses, and that it was not through any disrespect for the lieutenant colonel, or his authority, that I refused to comply with the order. A few high words followed, but Burgess only went on extra duty. The conversation between myself and the colonel was without auditors, save a negro cock, who started the report of our high words, which ran through camp like fire in dry stubble. That evening, after dismissal from dress parade, the boys of Company H caught me up and carried me to my quarters on the shoulders of several stout men, meanwhile cheering lustily. Orders from division headquarters were strict respecting the neat and soldierly appearance of pickets, guns bright, clothing brushed, and shoes blacked. In order to carry out this red-tape order, company commanders purchased blacking. But some of the boys found it difficult work to transform their worn and rusty shoes into anything like respectable coverings for the feet. W. Townsend, an excellent soldier, but somewhat eccentric, threw aside his badly worn shoes, and, as a burlesque on the order, took his place with the regular detail, his bare feet nicely blacked and polished to his contrasting white ankles, a roll or two in the bottom of his pantaloons making the contrast more conspicuous. Many of the men in line smiled, but Bill went through the ceremonies of inspection without any facial or other signs of knowledge of his clownish appearance. Lieutenant Colonel Mayhew, who appeared to know of no other mode of punishment, promptly had Townsend tied up by the thumbs with a guard to stand by him until his time expired. Captain Martin, passing by, saw the guard reach into Bill's pocket, take out his tobacco, and hold it to Townsend's mouth for him to get a chew. The captain then walked up, took out his knife, and cut the cord, and that was the last man of the Eighth that was ever tied up. This cruel and unauthorized mode of enforcing discipline would have been a dangerous undertaking in the command after that.

CHAPTER XI.

General Rosecrans, having his mind and heart set on Chattanooga, had by the 10th of August, 1863, repaired the Nashville Railroad as far as Stevenson, Alabama. Bragg was well known to be fortifying the "Gate City" of the South, whither he had retreated. Everything being in readiness for another general advance of the Army of the Cumberland, we received orders the 15th of August to march over the Cumberland Mountains. Accordingly, the Sixteenth (VanCleve's) Division broke up camp and took the Hill's Creek Gap road to Pikeville.

Before proceeding to give the details of our march over this rough country, a few words of explanation concerning the topography of this part of Tennessee will better enable the reader to understand our subsequent movements. The Cumberland Mountains consist of two ridges, divided for more than sixty miles by the narrow, fertile valley of Sequatchie. The high ridge east of the valley is called Walden's Ridge. This butts off against the Tennessee River, opposite a continuation of the same on the south side of the river, known as the Sand Mountains, which also abutt with towering cliffs on the south side of the river, leaving no space for a road, except by cutting a space into the sides of the bluff. Along the N. & C. R. R. has been made a rough wagon road, called the "Narrows." The Cumberland

Mountains proper slope from this narrow valley westward in broken bluffs for over forty miles, toward Middle Tennessee. Over these we were about to march.

The First and Second Brigades of VanCleve's Division (the Second under Colonel Barnes), passed through McMinnville, at noon, in the midst of a fierce rain storm. We only marched six miles and bivouacked at Harrison's Ford, of Collins' River. After wading the much swollen stream, by some error of the commissary all the commissioned officers were without a supply of provisions, taking all on hand to supply the soldiers for three days. Of course, the only alternative was to borrow at a usurious interest.

Early the 17th, we began the weary task of ascending the mountain, and was until noon in getting up the ammunition wagons, leaving the rear regiments to assist the artillerymen. We proceeded east, over a desperately rough road, twelve miles, to a small mountain stream, called Rock River, and bivouacked in a dense wood. Before dark, no less than six large rattlesnakes were killed by our regiment alone, and several by the Thirty-fifth Indiana and Twenty-first Kentucky. The fear of these poisonous reptiles caused our rest on the bare earth anything but pleasant. The men called this place Camp Snake.

After a hearty breakfast of crackers and coffee, with the luxury of a few potatoes, Captains Wilson, Wright and Dixon were appointed by Lieutenant Colonel Mayhew to search and overhaul the contents of our regimental wagons, and throw out all unauthorized baggage. To the great merriment of the men, the officers only found and threw out an old trunk, the property of one Hall, the wagoner whose complaints of overloading had caused the search to be made.

The 18th we marched to within six miles of the valley. We saw but few signs of civilization, the few houses that we passed being miserable looking cabins. The officers were worse off than the men for rations, but we managed to eke out enough for supper, with promise of some beef for breakfast.

About 10 o'clock the encampment had become comparatively quiet, men and officers lying asleep on the leafy ground, promiscuously. The drove of beeves the division quartermaster had brought over the mountain, from some cause, took fright, and broke from the corral and came crashing and tearing through the brush like a tornado, passing through the left of our regiment, frightening some of the slumbering soldiers so much, that many of them climbed saplings with the agility of squirrels.

At 9 o'clock, the 19th, we arrived at the precipitous descent to this beautiful, picturesque valley, which lay several thousand feet below us. We descended the road, or rather an irregular stone stairway, to the valley, then six miles up northward. We entered the ancient looking, mountain walled town of Pikeville, the inhabitants of which did not appear to be as proud to see us, as we had expected of Tennesseeans.

The following day was excessively hot, still many of the houses in this old, rusty looking town were closed, an evidence that the inmates were not overjoyed to see this first edition of Yankees. But the excessive heat, combined with female curiosity, overcame some of the inhabitants, and fair faces and well arranged toilets appeared at the front windows. At one sat the pretty Miss K, with rebellious heart and scorning black eyes, contemptuously cast at everything blue. Sergeant Hockersmith, of the Twenty-first, had a fancy for a well cooked mess of beef brains that amounted to almost a weakness, and was returning from the slaughter yard with his two brawny hands together, full of bloody brains. In passing the window the sergeant involuntarily turned his head to take a glance at so much beauty, beaming with wrath. With the quickness and spitefulness of a cat, she spit in the sergeant's face. A sudden movement, the brains were poised on the broad right palm, and sent flying through the open window at the young lady's face. Fortunately for her carefully arranged toilet, she had the discretion and activity to dodge the soft missile, which scattered over the nice carpet on to the opposite wall. The now furious sergeant strode on toward headquarters. Just then, an old, fat negro woman, in the brain bespattered room, exclaimed: " Dar, I'se tole Miss Sally she'd bring deaf an' destruction to dis here family yet." A short time after, a guard, accompanied by an officer, called on Miss Sally, and informed her that General V—— requested her presence at headquarters forthwith. The now frightened lady remonstrated with tears, but the captain of the guard gallanted her to the general's tent, followed by the old, fat darkey, who said: "I's gwine ter see what the great boss 'l do wid de chile." The general told her she was about as dangerous to the boys as a shell with a short fuse, and for safety to all parties, she had best go to her friends, outside the the pickets.

We remained at Pikeville until the 1st day of September, subsisting principally on green corn, sweet potatoes, and various other products, collected from the hitherto unmolested rich farms along the valley. Foraging parties were sent out daily from division headquarters, under command of commissioned officers, and our rudely-constructed tables were burdened with the good things of this favored region. In a few days after our arrival, the loyal East Tennesseeans began to come into our camp from their caves, dens, and hiding places in the mountains lying east and north of Sequatchie. The account some of these brave men gave of their hardships and hairbreadth escapes, told in their earnest, quaint manner, was indeed heroic and romantic. Some of them had dwelt principally since the summer of 1861 exiles from their homes and families. The most of them wore a haggard and careworn look, but the sight of the dear, old flag caused some to shed tears of joy. Among the latter was an old gray-haired Methodist preacher named Burkett. When he arrived in camp he was quite an object of pity.

He and the poor frame of a mule he rode were almost in a famishing condition. Lieutenant Colonel Mayhew recognized him as an old acquaintance, and made him a welcome guest in the Eighth. He proved to be a man of considerable talent and a pulpit orator equaled by few. He had been an intimate friend and co-worker of Parson Brownlow. We had him preach for us the night after his arrival, and there are few of the survivors of the Eighth but will remember the ragged old man's first sermon. His zeal for his Divine Master's cause was warm and earnest, but could not excel his patriotic enthusiasm for our bleeding country. By the time his sermon came to a close every man in the audience was a warm friend of old Brother Burkett, and a sum of money was immediately collected to buy him a suit of clothes. In a few days Colonel Price, of the Twenty-first Kentucky, had him commissioned chaplain of that regiment. Our newly appointed chaplain, Kindred, about this time arrived from Kentucky, and he and Father Burkett united their efforts for the promotion of the cause of religion in the brigade, and I am proud to record the fact that the able and untiring efforts of these good men did not prove fruitless.

General Rosecrans was completing his plans and movements for an advance on Chattanooga, the gate city of the Southern Confederacy. On the 21st August Colonels Wilder and Wagoner's cavalry brigades, with some of Wood's division of infantry, crossed over Walden's Ridge, via Poe's Tavern, opposite Thurman, and about the last of August shelled the city, to the great consternation of the inhabitants, as well as the rebels in arms, who made but slight resistance. The movement had the desired effect, i. e., to cause the enemy to leave some points below the city unguarded.

On the 1st of September we received orders, and marched down this peculiar valley, which is from two to four miles wide, and near sixty in length from north to south, fenced in by an almost impenetrable wall of mountains on either side. The dust was several inches deep, and the unclouded sun shone into this furnace-like valley with a fiery fierceness that caused our feet to blister, and the bugle call to halt for night was never before more welcome. Thus, for three days, we bore the heat and dust, and at last came in sight of Jasper, the county seat of Marion County, Tennessee. I was much amused at one of the Eighth boys, on coming in view of this irregular and rusty-looking town, saying, "I wonder if the town ain't yonder, among them old houses?" Our division camped here, and on the morning of the 4th a detail of one company from each regiment of our brigade was ordered to guard a large supply train, via Bridgeport, Alabama, to cross the Tennessee at that point. Company H, of the Eighth, in command of the author, composed part of this guard. While the men were preparing their breakfast, I told Scarbro to follow me, and proceeded to the brigade smith, who, with two hammers and cold chisel, followed the wondering Scarbro and myself to a deep ravine near camp, where the rivet in John's "jewelry" was quickly severed, and the dishonorable and galling irons were, by my order, cast into the weeds. I told the two men not to say anything about what became of the ball and chain. During the day many asked John where he kept his "jewelry." He invariably, replied, "I lost it, and ain't a going back to hunt fur it." The subsequent good behavior of Scarbro and courage displayed in action by him at Chickamauga probably saved me from a court martial.

On the morning of the 5th the long train crossed the swaying pontoon bridge at Bridgeport, Alabama, which had taken the place of the magnificent structure recently burned by the rebels. Company H's rations were about out, but circumstances favored these ever watchful boys of the Eighth, who discovered two of the bridge guards stealing each a side of bacon from one of the wagons while crossing the river. On reaching the southern shore they informed Captain Wright of the theft. That officer, who generally had an eye to the creature comforts of himself and men, returned with a squad of men, and soon had the coveted "ned" brought to light from one of the boats, and as the wagons were trundling ahead, I divided the bacon for more convenient transportation.

We had expected to join the division at Shell Mound, but on our arrival there, near sunset the 5th, we learned that the command had moved on. Early the next morning, Major Hoskins, commanding the guards, had the train in motion, but owing to the bad condition of the road up the river, around the foot of Sand Mountain (known as the "Narrows"), where many a stubborn and heroic army mule gave his life a sacrifice to our bleeding country, we did not come up with the main force until 10 o'clock, p. m., encamped in the mountains, eight miles from Trenton, Georgia, the county seat of Dallas County.

This country is very rough and mountainous. Old Carmoody, of Company H, "our Irishman," remarked, on the following morning, "Be jabbers, an' they hev so much counthry down here they jist hev to stack it up." What few of the inhabitants of this country we chanced to see were apparently ignorant and poor.

On the 8th we marched about four miles, over into Lookout Valley, and halted for further orders. Here four rebel deserters came to us and reported that General Bragg was about to evacuate Chattanooga, which proved to be a true report.

Quite early on the following morning we were marching on to Chattanooga, each soldier carrying sixty rounds of ammunition, feeling confident of engaging the enemy before night. At 9 o'clock we met a courier, with a dispatch stating that the enemy had evacuated. We soon struck the Trenton & Chattanooga Railroad, and with buoyant spirits pushed on down the railroad track and over the base of towering Lookout Mountain, from whence we could look down on the almost deserted little city, for many of the citizens had fled south at the approach of the "hateful Yankees." We passed on south of the city a few miles, and bivouacked at dark, near a few old houses the people called Rossville, having marched seventeen miles over very rugged roads. Weary and footsore, we lay down on the bosom of mother earth, with strong hopes of soon striking a death blow to the rebellion.

On the 10th, the division marched on the road toward Ringgold, the county town of Catoosa County, Georgia. Late in the afternoon our advance regiments ran into the enemy's pickets. After a short skirmish the enemy retired, and we again bivouacked for the night, with a strong guard thrown out, front and flank.

Early the 11th, our brigade, under command of Colonel Barnes, was put in advance. After passing the outer picket, Colonel Barnes ordered Companies A, B and F, of the Eighth, and three companies of the Fifty-first Ohio, forward as skirmishers, with the remainder of those two regiments forming line of battle on each side of the road, which ran through hills and hollows, heavily timbered, and covered with dense brush and undergrowth. The other three regiments composed the second line of battle. After advancing two miles, our skirmishers encountered the enemy's pickets, and commenced a brisk fire, the rebels gradually retiring. Notwithstanding the uneven country and dense brush, we maintained a good line, keeping close behind our skirmishers, who kept up a rattling fire on the retreating rebels, until they crossed East Chickamauga River, within three-fourths of a mile of Ringgold. They took a position on the east hill, which rises abrupt from the water's edge. The river, though a narrow stream, was in some places over six feet deep, and that, too, in good pistol range of the enemy's line on the hill above. Colonel Barnes said: " Boys, it's pretty steep, but we must make those scoundrels ' git.' By the right of companies, forward, march!" With a loud hurrah we plunged into the cold stream, regardless of wetting our few greenbacks, only endeavoring to keep our powder dry. The bullets pattered the water somewhat after the fashion at Stone River. We scrambled up the rocky hill under a shower of bullets, but, fortunately for us, the enemy's aim was generally too high in their first volley, and before they could reload our line was within a few yards of them, and they fled down the other side of the hill into Ringgold. Our few pieces of artillery were brought forward and shelled the town, while our line of battle continued to advance on quick time. On arriving in the suburbs, our progress was obstructed by light, paling fences. As each company neared one of these gardens or yards, a shout and simultaneous rush against these fences laid them as flat as if swept by a tornado. The terrified inhabitants were fleeing in every direction for safety from our noisy boys, who continued to fire at the armed rebels, whose flight through the streets was hastened by Colonel Wilder's mounted infantry, who came charging and yelling down the Knoxville road, trying to cut off their retreat. But we had pressed them too fast, and all but a few wounded and prisoners escaped, leaving us in possession of the town.

Our sudden and noisy entrance into this little aristocratic town spread great fear and consternation among the women, children and negroes, the principal inhabitants, as the chivalric gentlemen were in arms against their country. The former, who had never before seen any "Yankee vandals," had heard many horrible stories of our wanton cruelty, and no doubt now thought their time had come. An instance, witnessed by the writer, will give the reader some idea of many like scenes.

As Company H had just flattened out a paling fence, and passing in line through a nice yard, in which was a stately brick dwelling, over which our screeching shells were passing, a terrified woman, with five or six children, black and white, holding to her skirts, rushed out into the yard, in front of the advancing line, with her hands thrown up, imploringly addressed me thus: "Oh, what shall I do, sir!" I was about giving the command, "guide right," and added immediately, for answer to the woman, "into the cellar, I say." She replied: "Oh, but what will I do when you burn my house." I then added in a loud, imperative voice, and, pointing to the open cellar door with my drawn sword, "into the cellar, quick." The terrified woman and screaming little ones suddenly disappeared under ground, undoubtedly expecting soon to be roasted by the burning of her home.

We followed the retreating rebels, pursued by

Wilder, about three miles up the east fork of the Chickamauga, near Tunnel Hill, and bivouacked for the night. Before morning we learned that we were in close proximity to a large force of the enemy. We only had one man wounded. Wilder lost three killed. The enemy left several wounded in Ringgold. We subsisted that night on green corn and potatoes.

The 12th of September our division marched back to Lee & Gordon's Mills, on the west fork of the Chickamauga River. Our brigade was late at night in reaching camp, having to march in rear of a train and some beef cattle, we had captured from the enemy.

September 13th the sound of the bugle cut short our pleasant dreams. Shaking the cold dew from our gum blankets, we formed line of battle for one hour. Our advance had driven the enemy from this point the 11th, and from the wrecked appearance of the scattered rebel pay rolls, old trunks, officers' desks, etc., strewn over the ground, the Johnnies must have left suddenly while we were partaking of a breakfast prepared from the remnants of our previous day's allowance.

General T. Wood's division, on the opposite side of the river, was attacked by a rebel division. We hastily formed, and double-quicked over to his support. From the rattle of small arms the battle was hot, but was of short duration. Before we arrived Wood's men had run them off, but a rebel battery paid us a few compliments in the shape of some shell, that came uncomfortably near some of us. At 2 o'clock p. m. we re-crossed the river and rejoined the balance of Crittenden's Corps, occupying the same ground as we did the previous night.

September 14th. Reveille at 4 o'clock a. m., and orders to march at daylight. As usual, on such occasions, we had a hurried breakfast. Many were the different opinions expressed as to where and which way we would move next. It was generally known to our men that General Bragg was receiving large reinforcements from Richmond and Jo Johnston's army at Atlanta, and the boys said: "If we are to cross the river on the east side, there'l be some unpleasantness, sure." But at 8 o'clock the various arguments on that subject were unceremoniously cut short by General Crittenden marching us, with all the Twenty-first Corps, out on the road toward Chattanooga. After proceeding about five miles we halted in column, and remained there until dark. The men were allowed to sit or lie down, and those who mere fortunate enough to have any "grub" cooked got away with it.

When darkness began to spread over our wooded retreat we resumed the march, and moved to within one mile of Lookout Mountain, and bivouacked on a small hill in McLamore's Cove. This move was to form a closer connection with General Thomas, and await the tardy movements of McCook's Corps, having been sent around by Valley Head to cross Lookout Mountain at Stephen's Gap, and join the main army here.

The most of the Eighth lay down under their gum blankets to sleep without supper, and some were too hungry to sleep, but never too tired to grumble when their haversacks and stomachs were both empty. The writer lay for hours listening to the humorous discussions of the men on the wisdom or foolishness of this mysterious move. We at last slept, leaving the red signal lights still bobbing away on Lookout.

The "everlasting bugle," as the boys called it, awoke us at 4 o'clock, on the morning of the 15th. Soon the effects of so much promiscuous firing around the picket line began to come into camp in the shape of skinned hog, sheep, and occasionally a quarter of beef would come wagging in between two soldiers. It was a sweet and savory odor, eminating from hundreds of broiling steaks and frying mutton, whetting our already keen appetites. Soon full stomachs and cheerful faces took the place of sad, hungry men.

CHAPTER XII.

At 8 o'clock, on the morning of the 15th, the bugles sounded the assembly, and put a stop to our cooking and feasting, and at 9 o'clock the Twenty-first Corps was marching on the road to the noted Crawfish Spring, where we halted for one hour and filled our canteens from the fountain that forms the head of West Chickamauga River. Three miles further south we bivouacked near Owens' Mill, on East Chickamauga. Companies H and I were detailed from the Eighth for picket. We knew the enemy to be near our front, and great vigilance was therefore necessary, no fire or light being allowed at the reserve. But the night passed very quietly, except one alarm, caused by Gabbard, Company I, who fired at and badly crippled a cow that he had supposed to be a mounted rebel.

We remained here for three days, expecting an attack. The night of the 16th a reconnoitering party from the Eighth and Twenty-first Kentucky of sixteen men and two officers (Captains Wilson and Savage), crossed the river and silently crept through brush and thickets until they came near the enemy's cavalry videttes, two of them standing together. Captain Wilson, of the Eighth, heard them conversng, and crept near enough to hear them debating the probability of General Bragg and Longstreet's combined forces being able to utterly annihilate the

Union army under Rosecrans, in case they succeeded in cutting us off from Chattanooga.

The 17th, about noon, there was some firing between the enemy and Palmer's division, on our right. The morning of the 18th, two men of the Eighth, privates M. King and A. Logsdon, passed the pickets to go to Owens' Mill, to exchange some confederate scrip for some of the old fellow's black flour. When nearing the stream King discovered a rebel picket perched on the fence near the mill house. King stepped behind a tree and instantly fired, killing the Johnny. This was like stirring up a hornet's nest. The rebel skirmishers immediately commenced advancing, and opened on our line of pickets. In a few minutes a rebel battery from a hill near the mill opened on our camp. Artillery was hurried into position. Our pickets were reinforced and held them in check, but their shells played havoc with our coffee-pots, frying-pans, and a nice lot of beef the boys were jerking, as slowly drying it in strips was called by our negro cooks. One of the negro cooks snatched his coffee-pot from the fire and fled at the first shell. We hastily formed and took a position behind a slight eminence just in the rear of our bivouack fires. The pickets kept up a lively skirmish for several hours, the artillery from both sides throwing shells lively, theirs principally passing harmlessly over our line. At 5 p. m. we were relieved by Palmer's troops, and marched to Lee & Gordon's Mills, arriving there near 10 o'clock. Lieutenants Williams and Lewis and myself were debating ways and means for supper, as Bristo and Simp, with all the other colored cooks, had decamped, leaving us without supplies, when the white teeth and ebony countenance of Bristo appeared at our fire, still carrying his rescued coffee-boiler and contents that had been intended for our dinner. Lieutenant Lewis, in his joy at this lucky turn of affairs, said, "'Bris,' if this war ever ends, you shall have a pension for heroic conduct." Bristo replied: "Mars lieutenant, I's mighty feared dis nigger 'll end afoh de wah, ef I has ter stan' annuder sich a day."

It was now evident to all that a great battle was inevitable, and we rolled ourselves up in our gum blankets for a few hours' sleep, not knowing how many of our little regiment would sleep the sleep that knows no waking before the shades of another day closed around us. Hoping to be among those that would soon see the rebellion subdued into a lasting peace, that should be equally a blessing to North and South for many generations to come, we slept (after committing ourselves and our cause to Him who rules the destiny of nations) as sound as if no battle was pending or no danger near.

BATTLE OF CHICKAMAUGA.

The battle commenced about 8 o'clock, a. m., of the 19th, on the extreme left wing of our line. General Brannan's division of Thomas' corps, being stationed on the Lafayette road leading to Chattanooga, was first attacked, the firing rapidly increasing, and from that time until sunset was that continuous roar of firearms that speaketh death.

In order that the reader may have a better understanding of the position of the Eighth Kentucky, I will state the order of our line of battle. Next on the right of Brannan's division was Bird's division of the same corps; next was General Johnson's division of McCook's corps, and on the right of Johnson's was Palmer's division of Crittenden's corps, and next ours (VanCleve's division), and on our right Reynolds' division of Thomas' corps, which covered the ford at the mills of Lee & Gordon, with Wilder's cavalry guarding the extreme right wing. Our brigade, commanded by Colonel Barnes, was formed in column closed in mass. The colonel made us a short but thrilling speech, which I would reproduce here had I not lost my memoranda.

Our brigade was held in reserve near the river, below the mills, until near 2 o'clock, p. m. The superior numbers of the enemy enabled them to overlap with heavy force each division of ours as they attacked them in succession, and by noon the enemy had gained some advantage. Our right and center were being hard pressed. At 1 o'clock, p. m., they attacked Palmer's troops, and also overlapped them. Our division (VanCleve's) was then ordered in. Immediately in our front and between our lines and the enemy lay several hundred yards of dense undergrowth. We moved through this brush by the right of companies, then into line through a small cornfield to the edge of the heavy timber in which the enemy was posted. While crossing the field their skirmish line gave us a scattering fire, then hastily withdrew to their main line, not, however, until we captured several of them secreted behind a low rail fence.

We continued a steady fire on the enemy's line in our front. Our men appeared in the best of spirits, notwithstanding the heavy fire they were pouring on us. This continued for about thirty minutes, and the enemy's line appeared to be giving back. Several of our regiment had fallen, badly wounded, among them being B. Tudor, Company C. We were expecting momentarially to be ordered forward, when, to our surprise, we were completely flanked on our right by a heavy force, who opened an enfilading fire on us, at the same time those on our front opened with renewed vigor, this time with several pieces of artillery. We were ordered to fall back across the field to the thicket above mentioned, which we did in tolerable good order under a terrific storm of shot and shell, leaving many of our wounded comrades in that field. We, however, succeeded in carrying back with us Tudor, Company C, Logsdon and Webb, Company H, and several others. We straightened up our line under cover of the brush, and then by the help of part of Wood's Division succeeded in driving the enemy back to the timber. When night came on the firing ceased, except an occasional picket shot. It was with feelings of pride, blended with sorrow, that we re-formed our short companies of two dozen men each, in that thicket, preparatory to our second advance into the field. It was sad to see these brave boys, with clouded, but determined faces, the tears coursing down many of their powder-blackened cheeks, caused more from chagrin at being compelled to fall back than at the loss of comrades.

At dark, Colonel Barnes ordered Captain Wilson and myself with six men to carry a white flag into the cornfield after some of our wounded. A shower of bullets was the response. But we managed to get all of the Eighth off except those taken prisoners—Lieutenant-Colonel Mayhew and five men. By this inhumanity, the poor, suffering wounded of friend and foe continued their piteous cries and groans within easy hearing of both lines throughout the cold, frosty night. Never before did the horrors of war seem to us so cruel. We could distinctly hear their lamentable cries, "O, water, water!" and occasionally some poor, half-frantic sufferer calling the name of some familiar comrade or friend to come there. Though we heard none of the Eighth wounded that we could recognize, several of our brave boys ventured, after dark, to rescue some of the wounded of the Fifty-first Ohio. Considering the intense cold night, with our great coats and blankets far in the rear, our scant, poor rations, and being so near so much suffering humanity, without the privilege of giving any assistance, this certainly was the most miserable night the Eighth experienced during the war.

Early in the night, Company I, commanded by Captain Martin, was posted as pickets in an old field to the right of where our late engagement was, and he was relieved at midnight by the author with

Company H, of the Eighth. Two hours later, our entire force fell back two miles further toward Chattanooga. With such profound silence was this withdrawal made, that we, on the skirmish line, were not apprised of the move.

Darkness prevented any hostilities after 10 o'clock p. m. The enemy's pickets and ours were in close proximity. Their force in our front were busy chopping and felling trees the latter part of the night, making a great noise, and not until 4 o'clock a. m. on the 20th did we learn that the whole Union line had moved back over one and a-half miles, and the officer of the day had not yet notified me to fall back, and I did not intend to vacate without orders or a fight, and the latter event appeared certain as soon as the light of day appeared. I knew I could trust my company against any equal number of men and went along their line and instructed each, in case of being hard pressed, how to retire in line. The cold, frosty night made us shiver for overcoats. We were aware of our perilous condition, without any support, but coolly awaited events. About dawn, a heavy fog arose from the river and spread over the surrounding country. Under cover of this the rebel skirmish line withdrew, probably with the intention of being relieved by fresh pickets. They fell back over a small hill. At this time General Sheridan and staff passed in the rear of our little company of forgotten pickets. I sent Lieutenant Lewis to the road to hail the general. He gave me orders to withdraw my men immediately, adding that such gross neglect in a field officer of pickets should be looked into. My company retired in line until we cleared the open land, and then succeeded in joining the regiment, and while trying to boil some coffee for breakfast (our dusky cooks had not put in an appearance), we were ordered into line without the coveted coffee and "ned." Our brigade was detached from the division, and assigned a position near the center of the new line of battle, which was generally protected with slight and hastily-formed breastworks, made of rails, logs, stone or anything that could be conveniently had. The enemy's evident intention was to force their way between us and Chattanooga.

The battle was recommenced about 8 o'clock a. m., and by ten became furious all along the line. Col. Barnes was ordered to go to the support of one of General Thomas' divisions on the left center, who was being hard pressed. Hastily calling in our skirmishers, we double-quicked about one and one-half miles, halted, dressed up our line, and had just time to wipe the dust and sweat from our eyes, when two of our regiments, the 51st Ohio and the 8th Kentucky, were placed under command of Col. McLean, commanding the 51st, and ordered to go to the support of Gen. Rousseau, one-half mile further to the right. We resumed the double-quick, and passed down the rear of General Reynolds' regulars, who were busily engaged, pouring volley after volley into the rebel ranks, the balls of the latter making lively music about our ears. We entered a corn-field that had lately been laid waste, we being in column by companies. In our front, at the other side of the field, we saw the 15th Kentucky and two other regiments falling back, having exhausted their ammunition. The exulting rebels, under Breckenridge, were pressing forward, but not in very good order, though their bullets were making the corn-stalks rattle in a very unpleasant manner. Col. McL. gave the order, "On the right, into line, march!" This command was repeated by the clear, ringing voice of our young and gallant Major Clark. We executed this maneuver at the double-quick, with as much precision as we ever did on the drill-field. As soon as Rousseau's men had cleared our front, our boys opened "fire at will." When within sixty yards of the enemy, the order was given and repeated at the

After the words " memory recurs to it," 11th line from bottom of page 193, the following should appear:

When we were within twenty yards of the enemy they broke into a perfect rout. The Eighth Kentucky and Fifty-first Ohio boys kept up the charge, firing and re-loading as fast as expert hands could. We drove the enemy nearly half a mile, capturing two battle-flags and thirty prisoners. Our two regiments then took a position on the left of General Reynolds, and, during a lull in the continuous roar and rattle of small arms, our men labored hard in erecting a slight breastwork, gathering loose stones and logs. Up to this time neither army had gained any decisive advantage.

lately been laid waste, we being in column by companies. In our front, at the other side of the field, we saw the 15th Kentucky and two other regiments falling back, having exhausted their ammunition. The exulting rebels, under Breckenridge, were pressing forward, but not in very good order, though their bullets were making the corn-stalks rattle in a very unpleasant manner. Col. McL. gave the order, "On the right, into line, march!" This command was repeated by the clear, ringing voice of our young and gallant Major Clark. We executed this maneuver at the double-quick, with as much precision as we ever did on the drill-field. As soon as Rousseau's men had cleared our front, our boys opened "fire at will." When within sixty yards of the enemy, the order was given and repeated at the top of the voice of every captain: "Fix bayonets, charge!" The cheer the 8th Kentucky then gave, as we made that charge, will doubtless cause every surviving member's heart to swell with pride as often as memory recurs to it. But by some mistake of one of General Thomas' aids reporting to him that there was a gap in General Brannan's line (one of his brigades being in echelon caused this apparent opening), consequently General Wood was ordered to close up on Brannan's right. This move made an actual opening of a brigade's length in the line half a mile to our right. The enemy had, during the lull spoken of, been massing his forces on our right, and they took immediate advantage of the opening, charging into this gap with a powerful force, striking one brigade of Wood's division in flank, and sweeping it away, and also driving back the right of Brannan's line. Through this wide breach poured a long line of rebels, taking two batteries and instantly turning them on our right flank and the rear of General Reynolds' line, sending a perfect storm of grape and canister shot into our lines. At the same time we were in a brisk skirmish with the enemy in our front. This state of affairs made it impossible for us to hold our position many minutes without certain capture. Many of our noble boys were wounded. Private S. Lynch, Company K, was literally torn to fragments by a shell. Our retreat was necessarily a running the gauntlet between two fires, while the enemy was trying to close on us and cut us off. About twenty of the Eighth were captured, principally wounded.

Where a whole regiment, without a single exception, does its duty in an action, as our boys did here, individual mention, probably, should not be made; but the squad that stuck to Sergeant R. Cox and the flag, through the cornstalks, on this occasion, certainly deserve exceptional praise: Ab. Wiseman and W. Townsend, Company K; J. Tipton, Company C; P. Dennis, "Garl" Conner and C. Webb, Company H; Barnett and a few others. Tipton, Barnett and King were wounded and taken, but the other boys saved the flag. This coming under my immediate notice must be taken for my apology for especial mention.

The principal part of the Eighth, except those captured or wounded, rallied to the new line of battle, formed about a mile north of our former position, where we remained until 8 o'clock p. m.

At twilight on that bloody day a large rocket shot up from the enemy's line, and firing soon ceased. Our loss in this two days' battle was ten killed, forty-six wounded and twenty-four prisoners, most of the latter also wounded. Lieutenant Colonel Mayhew was captured the 19th. On the 20th Major Clark lost his horse and hat, and many of us had bullet holes in our clothing. That night all our army except Thomas' corps and the cavalry, made a silent, and, for many of us, a sad march to Rossville, four miles from Chattanooga, arriving there about 1 o'clock, a. m., the 21st. We threw our weary bodies on the ground, and for a short time became oblivious to the din, roar and clash of arms, but awoke at daylight, most of us feeling sore, with every limb and joint aching. The sad, powder-blackened faces of the men, their clothing torn into rags by the brush, some with pantaloons off at the knees, others without hats—all looking war-worn and brush-torn as they silently grouped around the bivouack fires, preparing our scant remnants for breakfast—would, under other circumstances, have caused mirth among ourselves at our own dilapidated appearance. But we could neither laugh nor ignore the fact, however, that for the first time we had left our helpless, wounded comrades on the bloody field in possession of the enemy. We all knew our army had defeated greatly superior numbers in their main object, i. e., to regain possession of Chattanooga, from which

Bragg's army had retreated eleven days before. We also knew that the enemy's loss in killed and wounded far exceeded ours, and they had gained only what they had before, and lost their boasted "gate city of the south."

CHAPTER XIII.

We arrived at Chattanooga at noon, the 21st of September, and were assigned our position on the extreme left wing of the new line near the Tennessee River, half a mile above the city. Though the Eighth boys were somewhat dispirited at our loss of comrades, they were not the kind of men to mope or entertain melancholly feelings. Every man in our army knew the great importance of holding the city, and, notwithstanding we had taken but three hours sleep within the last forty-eight hours, our bodies aching with pains from fatigue and hunger, as soon as the line of rifle pits were staked off the Eighth boys siezed picks and spades with eagerness, self-confidence and determination beaming from every face, vowing the rebels should never take the coveted city, and commenced heaving up the red earth, and to stimulate each other the boys assumed their wonted cheerfulness. The company commanders went into the city and each returned with several canteens full of whisky, captured from the enemy. The writer spent eight dollars for his company's spirits, and thought it was a good investment. The picks and shovels were not permitted to be idle a moment, day nor night. The Eighth officers would occasionally jump into the ditch and take some tired soldier's place, and allow him a few minutes rest.

By dark, the 22d, a line of good rifle pits extended for six miles in a semi-circle around the city, from our position to the mouth of the creek below the city.

The 23d, the enemy made their appearance on Mission Ridge. We expected an attack the next morning. That night the officers and men labored hard, carrying small trees and brush from the river bank, forming an entanglement in front of our works. We also stretched a telegraph wire, about one foot above ground, secured to strong stakes, among the brush in our front, intending to trip up and confuse the attacking rebels, should they charge our works. But the threatened attack was never made. Their line of pickets was established east of Citico Creek, along the foot of Mission Ridge.

The 25th of September, our pickets being much annoyed by some rebel sharpshooters, concealed in a house east of the creek, one of our batteries at Fort Wood sent a few explosive shells over. One of them went crashing through and fired the building. About twenty Johnnies left there quite suddenly, and our men could raise their heads above the edge of the picket holes without so much danger. Soon after this, the enemy's pickets lying in hailing distance of ours, agreed to cease hostilities, unless either should advance. This was a private's affair, but was maintained with few exceptions for several weeks. However, the rebels would insist on the fun of shooting at our officers when they came near our line. We often took advantage of them by swapping coats with the men, and carrying a gun, and no sword. On one of these occasions the writer heard the following conversation between a rebel picket and one of the Eighth.

Rebel Picket.—" You'ens got plenty of coffee over thar?"

Eighth Picket.—" You are mighty right, we have."

R. P.—" How'll you swap for some Kentucky whisky?"

E. P.—" Pint for pint; come over."

They met each other half way, without arms. After each had taken a drink and exchanged exhilarating stimulants, the Eighth picket said:

" How many men had Bragg in the fight, last week?"

R. P.—" Some sixty thousand. How many was they of you'ens?"

E. P.—"Oh, about thirty thousand."

R. P.—" See here, Yank, that's too thin; you'ens wus more'n we'ens."

Then each returned to his post.

With the kind reader's permission, we will look at another scene in army life, in strange contrast to the bloody scenes we have just recorded.

Time, the 28th of September. Darkness is spreading over the camp and surrounding country. The numerous camp fires of the enemy are twinkling for miles along the west side of Mission Ridge, and the bright full moon is just looming up over the host of the enemy. The last notes of the bands of the various headquarters are dying in echoes up the broad Tennessee. The rough, war-worn veterans of the Eighth and Twenty-first are collecting in a circular crowd. Chaplains Kindred and Burkett are about to commence divine worship, some of the men seated on the ground, some on cracker boxes or other hastily improvised seats. In the midst rises an aged, white-haired man with open book in hand. A lighted candle in a bottle, placed on a pile of cracker boxes, complete the pulpit arrangements. None in camp are yet asleep, but unusual quiet pervades. The joker has hushed, all profanity ceases. The aged man lines the hymn, "Ashamed of Jesus." The soldier audience join in the song, their clear, rich voices ring far out over the placid river. Then follows an able, earnest petition to the throne of God for fallen humanity and our suffering country. Then the refugee preacher holds his male auditors in rapt attention for more than an hour, dwelling at some length on the wickedness of the rebellion. As the old man warmed up on this subject, the peculiar curl of his thin lip grows sharper, his grey eyes kindle to fiery orbs, his gesticulations grew more animated, and his countenance more furious. With arms flung on high, as if grasping after a thunderbolt to hurl at the leaders of the rebellion, he drew a picture of their crimes in appalling colors, describing the dreadful horrors of this useless destruction of young lives. At last the speaker descends from his thunder tones, and his voice wailed out such pathetic sorrow for our dead, and suffering wounded, as to cause the unaccustomed tears to glisten on many bronzed cheeks, winding up with a prayer to God, "if possible, to forgive the very leaders of the rebellion," and to enable our army to save the country and restore the Union. Silence taps is sounding and the grand old song, "Praise God from whom all blessings flow," is sang with a new meaning to many.

Owing to the difficulty of wagoning supplies over the mountains from Bridgeport, Alabama, the army only received half rations, and that, too, of a very inferior quality. Our boys began to study ways and means to supply the much needed grub.

Sergeant Hironmus, Company D, a brave and adventurous, but quiet and cautious, man, while on picket had observed that the enemy daily drove a large herd of Texas cattle from the corral to the river, near the pickets, for the purpose of watering them. He also observed that the careless, cowardly herders frequently allowed the hungry kine to scatter along the river bank, browsing on the green cane. Frank said nothing, but on the morning of the 7th he ordered out a foraging party composed of Sergeant Hironmus, commanded by said Sergeant, clad in a rusty, dilapidated suit of butternut jeans. He took his trusty old squirrel rifle, which he had found somewhere in Dixie, and, under cover of the heavy fog, crept along the river bank, protected from the view of the pickets by the heavy growth of cane and weeds, and secreted himself inside the enemy's lines until thirteen head of cattle had passed below him.

He then managed to give his hat a wave on a stick, poked out from his hiding place. The frightened cattle did not stop until inside our lines, where they were soon converted into beef for our brigade. The next day the Confederacy lost several more nice cattle, branded C. S. After that their pickets were strengthened near the river, and we got no more Texas beef.

The 10th of October our encampment was visited by Generals T. L. Crittenden and VanCleve. They both bade us farewell. Our men expressed some surprise, and much regret, at thus giving up our corps and division generals.

The next evening, at dress parade, the following address was read by the adjutants of each regiment in the Twenty-first Army Corps, which lost its designation as such by being blended with, and became a part of the Fourth Army Corps:

CHATTANOOGA, October 10th, 1863.

To the Officers and Soldiers of the Twenty-first Army Corps:

The general commanding announces with sorrow that the name of this corps has been stricken from the army rolls, and that he has been relieved from duty and ordered to report at Indianapolis, that his conduct in the late battle of Chickamauga may be investigated. The general regrets the separation, and not the investigation. The closest scrutiny, however it may effect him, can only brighten your future. Your deeds at Chickamauga, as at Stone River, will hand down to posterity your honored names. You have honored me. The mighty hand of the Twenty-first Army Corps has graven the name of its commander on the famous pages of the past, and the slanderous tongue cannot revoke that past. Further honors await you. May God's blessings attend you.

T. L. CRITTENDEN, *Major General*.

The Third Brigade, to which the Eighth belonged, was assigned to the command of General Wat. Whitaker, of the Sixth Kentucky, and Colonel Barnes again took command of the regiment. About this time the officers of the regiment made and forwarded a petition to General Thomas, who had superseded General Rosecrans, asking for the consolidation of the Eighth Kentucky into a battalion of five companies. This was done on account of the reduced number of men in each company, not averaging over fifty each.

On the 18th of October a detachment of one hundred and seventeen men and four officers were detailed from the brigade, and sent, under command of the writer, to the general field hospital, in Spring Valley, on the north side of the river. Thirty-two of these men were from the Eighth Kentucky. This detail remained there until the 1st of November, doing fatigue duty of various kinds, chopping wood, putting up hospital tents, making bunks, gathering forest leaves for beds, digging graves, burying the dead, and caring for the necessities of the wounded.

The 23d of October the Eighth moved to the north side of the river, into Moccasin Bend, opposite Lookout Mountain, were they commenced to prepare winter quarters. The men went to work with their axes, preparing material, trying to be cheerful with the scant half rations.

About the 27th General Hooker's forces, from the Potomac, arrived in Lookout Valley, and attacked the enemy at Wauhatchie on the 28th, and after a hot engagement succeeded in driving the enemy south of Lookout Creek, and made connection with our army by a pontoon bridge, near the foot of Sand Mountain.

The hospital fatigue party were especially busy when the ambulances conveying Hooker's wounded began to arrive, bearing over two hundred mangled, bleeding and suffering men. A few of them were rebels, who received the same care as our own men. There was a general moving around of the wounded to make room for those coming in, twenty dead to bury, with a prospect for twenty more in a few hours. These hard worked and poorly fed duty men complained to the writer for more grub or less work. I had used all my pursuasive powers to induce Boughton, the quartermaster, to increase rations for these duty-men, but without effect. I called up six of the Eighth and four of the Fifty-first boys, and told them and Lieutenant Cassidy, of the Thirty-fifth Indiana, that if there was any animal fit for human food within ten miles of camp, I knew they were the men that could find it, and whether it belonged to friend or foe, to have it there before night. Just after dark the foragers returned, each two of the squad bringing in a part of a beef. Before morning the other half was brought in and given to the wounded and waiters. Doctor Perkins, surgeon in charge, thankfully received a good roast, and commended my course, but had too great fears of red tape to take the responsibility of ordering out a foraging party. I told him if the government would not or could not feed my men, they should be allowed to feed themselves.

We found only one of the Eighth boys in the general field hospital. Presley Sloan, Company D, had been knocked senseless by a piece of shell on the evening of the 20th of September. The leaves that had drifted where he fell caught fire, and burned the skin from his entire body. He said that he had suffered terribly, but was in a fair way of recovery. A very sad case of destitution, caused by war, was that of Mr. Powell, who, with his wife and six children, were hovering under a few old pieces of tents and quilts, near our encampment. They had fled from their burning dwelling during the battle of Chickamauga, penniless, roofless, and nearly friendless. One of his little boys died a few days after our arrival at the hospital, and some of our boys made a rude coffin and buried him for the stricken parents.

The 31st of October the brigade received orders to march. Our fatigue duty-men were ordered back to their respective regiments, and the 1st of November, with some reluctance, we left our half finished cabins. Some of the men said, "If we're going where we can get full rations once more, it is all right."

When we arrived at headquarters the 1st November, tents, camp and garrison equipage, officers' baggage, including desks, company books, &c., were packed into a pile, a guard detailed and left to guard them, and the brigade marched to the river, where we had to wait three hours for repairs to the pontoon bridge, which had been damaged by large rafts of logs set adrift by the rebels. We then marched single file over the treacherous, swaying bridge, and run the gauntlet up through Lookout Valley, under fire of the enemy's heavy guns stationed on the northwest slope of Lookout Mountain. None of the brigade, however, were hurt. We bivouacked at Wauhatchie, the numerous fires of the enemy twinkling like stars on frowning Lookout. At dark, Colonel Barnes received information that the enemy was advancing on us. All our cheerful camp fires were reluctantly extinguished, and we lay in line of battle during the night, ready for any emergency. We were not attacked, but spent a sleepless night. At sunrise we ate a hasty breakfast, and marched over a spur of Raccoon Mountain and down Clearwater Creek. My company, on duty as train guard, was, at dark, a long way behind the regiment, caused by bad roads and broken down wagons.

The night of the 2d November, 1863, found us back at Shellmound, Tennessee, where General Whitaker informed Colonel Barnes we would fortify and go into winter quarters. From this time until the 12th we suffered much from the inclemency of the weather, having left the remnant of our old tents at Moccasin Bend, and most of the men's overcoats and blankets were still boxed up at Nashville, where they were sent in the spring by general orders. The nights were cold for this climate, but the men of the Eighth were not the men to sit still and freeze or starve without an effort to remedy the evil. Procuring as many axes as could be had, logs were cut and large fires built, around which the men at night collected, sung their songs, and joked each other about their ragged appearance, with as much cheerfulness as if we were in the best of barracks. Sergeant Wood remarked: "I can stand a heap if they will only feed me well." We were kept too busy during these days to feel the cold. Cutting down trees and building fortifications occupied part of our time the first two weeks here. A large part of each regiment was detailed to cut trees and prepare material for our winter quarters. A daily guard of forty men was furnished by our brigade to escort provision trains to Whiteside's Station. The horrible condition of the road through the "Narrows" made it hard work helping wagons out of mud holes, but supplies for a large army at the front could not be neglected.

The 9th, Colonel Barnes, Major Clark and Captain Powell laid off our new encampment. Chaplain Kindred, Captain Dixon and myself were appointed by the colonel to take charge of and superintend the building parties. Our men worked under many disadvantages for want of axes. This was soon remedied by borrowing from the division quartermaster, and a few old cross-cut saws, gathered up from the surrounding neighborhood. Thus work on our cabins progressed daily.

CHAPTER XIV.

About the 15th of November General Sherman's army began to pass up the river road, toward Chattanooga, and we all expected more "unpleasantness" with the Johnnies soon.

The 18th our brigade was reviewed by General Whitaker. Our lines were much shorter than twelve months ago, but in marching past old " Wat," he raised his hat, and said : " Colonel Barnes, that regiment of yours is an honor to our state. Gad, but they can march without music as well as with it."

The next day the ever welcome face of the paymaster appeared, and we received our allowance of greenbacks for September and October. That night, after all had retired with full pockets, orders came to prepare to march, but recent rains had rendered the bad road almost impassable, and the rear of Sherman's force had not cleared the Narrows, therefore we did not move until the morning of the 23d.

The 22d the colonel and Captain Smallwood had a few short words, resulting in the latter being put under arrest. After a hard day's march, with sixty rounds of cartridges and four day's rations, we halted for the night at the base of Mount Raccoon, opposite to and west of frowning Lookout, on whose summit and western side the enemy's numerous camp fires twinkled like stars in the black, distant horizon. Every man in our army, from a private to General

Grant, knew it would be a desperate undertaking to drive the Johnnies from that mountain. Its maintainance was of vital importance to them, therefore they had fortified this naturally strong position, wherever the best of military skill of the rebel officers thought would add to its defense. But the possession of Lookout was also of great importance to the Union army, and General Grant said it must be taken. We lay down to rest our weary bodies, for the hazardous undertaking before us. Early on the morning of the 24th our brigade of the Fourth Corps, joined Slocum's troops of Hooker's Corps, and moved up Lookout Valley into a dense forest, south of the Wauhatchie, where the enemy lost sight of us for a few hours.

Captain Smallwood's company (K) sent a polite request to Colonel Barnes that they desired their captain's release from arrest, and that he be permitted to command them in battle. The request was at first refused. Then Smallwood appealed to General Whitaker, who rode up to Colonel Barnes, and said: "Colonel, this captain is only under arrest for some petty personal slang you and he have been indulging in; now, by G—d, he is too brave an officer to miss this engagement. It will be an honor to you to overlook the matter, and restore him his sword and command." It was done, and no more was heard of court martialing Captain Smallwood.

In this forest we piled our knapsacks, blankets, and part of our rations, and left them under a guard.

We filed off to the left, crossed Lookout Creek on an old mill-dam, and commenced the difficult task of ascending the mountain through a thicket of cedars, that skirted the base of the mountain. Up, still up, meeting with no opposition, except inanimate nature, pulling up by shrubs and projecting rocks. At last we reached the inaccessible wall of limestone, a perfect palisade, several hundred feet high. This movement was still unobserved by the enemy, who were expecting us to attack them in front. We faced north, the Eighth Kentucky forming the extreme right wing of the line, therefore we were nearest the cliff. A heavy skirmish line was put forward. We moved forward, keeping well up with our skirmishers. Thus we swept along the steep, rugged mountain side, over huge rocks, fallen trees and deep ravines, regardless of the scattering shots sent at us from the mountain top. The labor was severe. Soon every man, including our brave, old fat colonel, was wet with perspiration. A heavy fog, that hovered over the mountain, enabled us to take the enemy by surprise, in the flank and rear of their works. Their evident confusion was so great that they made but a feeble, unorganized resistance, their defense being principally Indian fighting, from behind trees and large rocks. We gleaned a rich harvest of prisoners, and several pieces of artillery, principally from Stevison's Division. Those of the enemy that were not captured fled around the nose of the mountain, and took a strong position on the southeastern slope, just under the towering cliff. About this time two of our heavy seige guns on Moccasin Point opened fire, and were replied to by those of the enemy, on point of Lookout, almost immediately over our heads. By this time, 3 p. m., a dense cloud enveloped the mountain, and the battle which followed has passed into history as "the battle above the clouds." The enemy made a determined stand, as they were strongly reinforced in their fortified new position. A good many of the Eighth having been sent back to Lookout Valley, in charge of prisoners, we were left in reserve on the "nose" of the mountain, and being near the wall or palisade, the enemy above us not only shot at us whenever the cloud would lift, so as to enable them to see, but resorted to a novel method of warfare, rolling down loose stones at us. Under cover of the fog, a few of our sharpshooters took positions, concealed behind trees and large stones, and soon picked off every Johnnie that dared to show his head on top of the cliff. Though their ordinance made a terrific noise, their heavy missiles passed harmlessly over our heads, as their pieces could not be depressed to a sufficient angle to reach us. During the evening, and to a late hour of the night, a heavy battle was fought, as it were almost under our feet. Our forces succeeded in driving the enemy around the mountain to the Summertown road, and at 10 o'clock the struggle ceased, the union forces expecting to renew the conflict at daylight. Four of the Eighth were wounded by balls, and several injured by rocks, rolled at us from above. None were dangerous wounds. As usual, every man in the regiment and brigade did his whole duty. B. F. Ward, Company F, an excellent shot, succeeded in silencing a particularly annoying rebel sharpshooter, who had secreted himself in a niche of the irregular crown of the precipice. The rapidity of his shots were only accounted for by his comrades behind loading for him. Ben maneuvered until he obtained a position commanding a view of the annoying rebel's head. As the fog lifted above the mountain, Ben's unerring rifle cracked. The rapid shooter sprang forward, and fell on a ledge of rock twenty feet below. His hat, with a bullet hole in it, came to the base of the cliff. Ben lay there a long while, but no other daring rebel showed his head at that point.

There was a sudden change in the temperature of the atmosphere at the close of this eventful and historic day. Within a few hours the sultry, damp air had lowered to nearly zero. We felt this change more sensibly on account of having exerted ourselves in the charge on the mountain side, heating our blood, and having our clothing wet with perspiration. Thus, in our exalted position, without blankets, great coats or fire, our suffering during the night can better be imagined than described. Sleep was among the impossibilities. But not a murmur was heard from these brave men. The life or death of the cause of freedom and good government was in the scale, and outweighed any bodily suffering of a few hundreds or thousands of men. In our silent and shivering vigils of the night, we could occasionally hear a heavy, rumbling noise on the top of Lookout above us, that caused us pickets to suspect some movement of the enemy. In the early dawn of the 25th, Gen. Wat. Whitaker walked up in front of the 8th Kentucky, and said, "Col. Barnes, I want a few volunteers to climb that cliff and see if the enemy are still there." The Colonel replied, "The whole regiment, General, if you wish it." Every man sprang to his feet, ready to obey the expected command. But only Capt. Wilson and six picked men were permitted at that time to immolate themselves on this high altar as a sacrifice to our country's cause. These apparently devoted men, carrying the 8th's flag, proceeded to ascend this hundred feet or more of almost perpendicular wall, at a place where there was an irregular kind of a natural stairway, by which hung a large wild grape vine. At the base stood the 8th, and with bated breath we watched this brave little squad, with their guns slung over their backs, climbing to where, in all probability, sudden death awaited them. At last they disappear over the top. Hearing no noise above us indicating the presence of the enemy, we instantly commenced the toilsome ascent of Lookout in the same manner the squad had just done.

Just as the king of day came peeping up over Missionary Ridge, Capt. John Wilson stepped out on the projecting brow of Lookout Mountain, and unfurled to the morning breeze that dear old emblem of light and liberty. As the sight of the flag met the upturned gaze of our vast army below, cheer after cheer echoed and re-echoed from camp to camp, from mountain to mountain, until the bosom of the placid, broad Tennessee River and the beautiful valleys appeared to shout for very joy. The enemy during the latter part of the night had silently fled from their works, both on top and along the south-east side of Lookout, and joined the balance of Bragg's army on Mission Ridge, leaving over 200 of their sick and convalescent, with a thin line of pickets surrounding their camp at Summertown, half a mile west of the point of Lookout.

As soon as the 8th reached the top, we hastily marched out to Summertown, where the scared and sickly looking pickets surrendered to us without even firing a gun. We also captured a large quantity of corn meal, twenty barrels of very dirty sugar, two wagon loads of "rebel crackers," apparently of a mixture of ground peas, middlings or fine saw-dust, and of adamantine hardness. Also forty large Marquee tents were among the Quartermaster's stores that fell into our hands, and provided us shelter the week we remained on the top of this high, cold mountain. As Gen. Hooker rode up to us (via the Summertown road), Gen. Wat. Whitaker addressed old "Fighting Joe" thus: "General, as the 8th Kentucky had the courage to come up here first, I hope you will let the Regiment remain here and guard these stores and this position." This modest request Gen. Hooker readily granted, remarking, "Sir, these western soldiers will fight anything on earth like rebels, and even climb above the clouds to complete victory and capture the enemy." The 96th Illinois, commanded by Col. Champion, was ordered up, and joined the 8th in throwing a line of earthworks near the point or nose of the mountain.

On this 25th November, 1863, our first day on Lookout, we were eye witnesses of one of the grandest, most gigantic and exciting battle scenes that took place during this or any other war. From our high position we could overlook the country to a much greater distance than our natural vision could reach. The city of Chattanooga lay almost under us. Our vast army of nearly one hundred and twenty thousand men, stretched away southward, in dark blue lines, in the valley. Parallel to those living lines, stretches this peculiar ridge, where the enemy in strong force were well fortified, with months of incessant and well directed labor, engineered by the best of military skill, was added to this already natural strong position. Behind these with their hundreds of heavy guns, we do not wonder the rebels felt confident of repulsing any force that could assail them. When Sherman's forces began to warm up the Johnnies near Fort Buckner into a smart battle, many of the officers and men of our two regiments seated themselves on the crowning rocks of the precipice to view for our first time a great battle at a safe distance. I was the fortunate owner and possessor of a double lens opera glass, with the aid of which I could see the buttons on a man's coat at a distance of five miles. Thus situated the whole panorama of the great battle of Mission Ridge, with all its harrowing details, passes under our view, except some of the assaults made in the forenoon by Corse's and Lightburn's Brigades on the northern slope of Tunnel Hill, on which was situated Fort Buckner, on which Sherman's batteries near the river and those near Orchard Knob, were showering their shot and shell with great rapidity and effect. While our batteries in Forts Wood and Thomas were lively in their respects to Fort Bragg, situated near the center of the rebel line, about 11 a. m., a brigade of Sherman's troops made a charge on the west slope of Tunnel Hill. The enemy being entrenched withstood them for a while, mowing down hundreds of these brave men. The line pushed up, leaving the hill side strewn with dead and wounded. We could see some dragging their mangled bodies back down the slope, while their more fortunate comrades were mounting over the rebel works and the Johnnies fleeing to the shelter of Fort Buckner. At last Sherman had, by persistent pounding on the rebels' right, succeeded in drawing reinforcements from their center, and we could see the head of Hooker's column ascending the slope, away to the right, near Rossville.

At two o'clock p. m. there had been a slight cessation of the contest and roar of artillery. Six of our heavy siege guns, fired at intervals of two seconds, the signal for the starting of the Fourth Corps to assault Fort Bragg. The long blue lines sprang at once to their feet, and our vast army made a simultaneous forward movement one and a half miles to the foot of the bridge. The rebel artillery, consisting of hundreds of guns, sent storms of bursting shells far out over the valley, specking the air like mammoth snowflakes, all our heavy artillery returning the fire, which made the mountains fairly tremble with their terrific thunder.

At the foot of the ridge, our troops encountered a rebel earthwork, packed with the enemy, and rimming it like a battlement. This was carried almost without a halt. But we could see our men falling thick and fast as they neared these works. And as they cleared them the rebel prisoners came streaming back, unarmed, toward the city, like the tail of a kite, running for their lives to escape the destructive missiles of their friends. While the noble old Fourth Corps struggled on up in the face of shot and shell, Hooker's men, near Rossville, were swinging around to flank the enemy's works. As the long blue lines of the Union forces ascended nearer the top, the sixty guns in the rebels' thirteen batteries concentrated their fire upon the assaulting lines. But now to reach them, they could not depress their cannon sufficiently. They cut the fuse of their shells shorter and shorter, while their rifle pits were ablaze with fire of small arms. It did not seem possible to us that our men could live to reach the works, for in addition to this murderous fire, the rebels began to roll down huge rocks and shells with lighted fuse. But these heroic men had served too long under "old Lion Heart" to waver only for a few minutes. As they did so, and we could see behind them the hundreds of prostrate comrades, our hearts appeared to be ready to leap out of our throats. I am confident my hair more than once came near pushing my cap from my head. But onward and upward they clamber, and the brow of the ridge is reached, then the fighting is more like demons than men. Many of the veteran rebels stood at bay like gray wolves. This could not last long. We wiped the briny liquid from our eyes, and could see the enemy flying over the eastern slope of the ridge, with their own deserted artillery playing upon them. The enemy were routed completely. The men of the Eighth cheered, slung their hats, and gave every expression of joy. Some danced, while the tears of joy rolled down their cheeks. Big Sergeant Bain, of Company A, said to me, after giving me a rib-crushing hug, "Cap., that sight's wuth more'n all my wages; it's just awful grand, but powerful dangerous work."

On the 26th, Colonel Barnes, in compliance with orders from General Thomas, distributed the tents and commissaries captured on the mountain, with General Geary's division of Hooker's corps. We found the C. S. crackers a poor apology for bread—could not be eaten without soaking. Then one cracker would swell to a spongy, tasteless mass of gluey, slimy stuff, revolting both in looks and smell. The meal and sugar, though dirty, were palatable.

We remained here, with little or nothing to do but eat and digest our poor grub, until the 2d day of December, when we received the welcome order to return to our winter quarters at Shell Mound, Tenn.

The Eighth arrived at our quarters at Shell Mound,

the evening of the 3d of December. A general good and cheerful feeling appeared to pervade the entire command. This was augmented by the arrival of our much needed blankets and overcoats.

"Now," as one of the boys said, "we have run old Bragg and his bragging crowd off, I reckon they will let us have time to finish our cabins." Every officer and man went to work with a will, and we soon completed our little, neat and well laid off town, each cabin containing one mess of six men.

On the 6th, the brigade was reviewed by General Whitaker, and the 7th he started to his home in Kentucky. Colonel Barnes took command of the brigade, and Major Clark command of the Eighth Kentucky.

The 10th we received the long looked for order to consolidate the regiment into a battalion of five companies. General Stanley, division commander, appointed a board of officers to examine and decide upon the commissioned line officers' qualifications, and decide who should be retained in service.

The 15th of December this board met, consisting of Colonel Walters, Nintieth Ohio; Lieutenant Colonel Cummings, Ninety-ninth Ohio; Captain Sergent, Fifty-first Ohio, and two captains of the Twenty-fourth Ohio. This board proceeded to make a separate examination of one hour, of each of the ten captains, on tactics, regulations, guard and picket duty, and all other military duties incumbent on a company commander. On the next day the board convened again, and called for the following named captains: Wilson, Wright, Benton,

Ketchins and Smallwood. Colonel Walters addressed us thus: "Well, gentlemen, you are the five captains that we have decided upon as most efficient, and you will therefore remain in command. The board then requested that each of us write down the names of five lieutenants of each rank, as we were acquainted with their circumstances and qualifications, to guide them in their selections. After considerable hesitation we each made a list, without consulting each other, and handed them to Colonel Walters, and then retired. The board decided that First Lieutenants W. Park, Harklerhodes, Williams, N. Jones and J. Phipps, and Second Lieutenants C. Park, G. W. Lewis, J. S. Tye, J. Pucket and J. McGuire should be retained in service. All the other officers, including Colonel Barnes and Major Clark, were by reason of this consolidation discharged, and started for their homes in Kentucky, the 23d of January, 1864. Captain John Wilson and the men that first topped Lookout on the 24th of November, at the same time received a thirty days' furlough, and accompanied the supernumerary officers home. The following are the names of this brave squad: Sergeants Joseph Wages, Charles Witt, Ed. Anderson, privates William Witt and John Gilbert. We felt sad at parting with these brave and genial brother officers, with whom we had been intimately associated for over two years, and in that time had together braved so many dangers, endured so many hardships, and passed so many pleasant hours together, and especially did we regret to lose the ever cheerful company of Major Clark, who, on the evening previous to starting home, attempted to read his farewell address to the regiment at dress parade; but his emotions overcame his utterance, and the reading of the following farewell address was concluded by Adjutant Park :

Officers and Soldiers of the Eighth Kentucky Volunteers :
This regiment having been by the casualties of the service reduced to less than half the maximum number prescribed by law, is consolidated to a battalion of five companies, as provided for in General Orders No. 86, of the War Department; therefore my connection with the regiment and army ceases. In parting with you, I tender you all my sincere thanks for the cordial support you have at all times given me, both as an adjutant and, subsequently, major of the regiment. My association with you in the service for over two years has created within me a brotherly affection for you, which has been prompted and authorized by your uniform courtesy and kindness toward me. Your willingness and readiness at all times to obey lawful orders, have not only excited my admiration, but the admiration of all your officers with whom you have been connected. In the history of this war the first word to your dishonor remains to be written. The coolness and gallantry you evinced at Snow Hill, Dobbin's Ferry, Stone River, Chickamauga, and at Lookout Mountain, do not foretell ought of dishonor that would cloud the bright name the Eighth has won. Those who participated in battles for the Union's restoration, both living and dead, will be remembered and honored by the grateful and patriotic people as long as the horrors of this accursed rebellion are remembered and deplored. In relinquishing the command of the regiment, I hope and believe that you will give Captain Wilson, a good and gallant officer, that co-operation which you have hitherto so generously extended to me. May God watch over and protect you all.
JOHN S. CLARK, *Major Commanding.*

The writer would be glad to insert Colonel Barnes' farewell address, but has been unable to procure a copy. But the Major's farewell will convey to the reader's mind some idea of the warm friendship that existed generally in the command.

CHAPTER XV.

About the 25th of December, 1863, the United States Government offered to all able bodied soldiers who had served two years or more a bounty of four hundred dollars, and a thirty days' furlough to re-enlist as veteran volunteers, and serve three years from re-enlistment, or during the war, the remaining part of the first enlistment to be served out in their present organizations. During the last week in the departing year re-enlisting in the Thirty-fifth Indiana and Twenty-first Kentucky was lively, but the Eighth boys only talked and joked each other about becoming "veterans."

The night of the 24th of December many of the Eighth boys thought to have some old fashioned Christmas guns, having saved a quantity of powder for that purpose. Many beer bottles exploded in their buried security from sight, but not from sound, and the officer of the day, at the urgent command of Colonel Barnes, called out the camp guards to suppress the Christmas guns, which only partially succeeded. But the next night afforded the boys a chance for some amusement at the expense of a few tony officers. A rebel captain's wife, named Burnett, living not far from our picket line, gave a party of United States officers, and about a dozen of the most aristocratic young ladies in that neighborhood, a supper. Captain Temple, our brigade commissary, and a few other officers, furnished the material for the principal part of the supper. A party of sergeants and privates of the Eighth and Twenty-first Kentucky, after dark, obtained the countersign, and slipped out to the house where music and dancing, as well as feasting, was the principal programme. The boys succeeded in placing a good many of their yet unexploded bottles of powder under and around the house. As the fuse to each were of good length, the boys were well concealed before those bottles and that ball exploded. In a few minutes not a girl could be found inside the enclosure, but many were seen running through the fields as if the day of doom had surely come. No person was hurt, but many were scared.

The last few days of December were warm and rainy, especially the 31st, when the rain fell in torrents until late in the evening, when the wind suddenly veered to the north, and grew in cold and power. Our boys on picket, with soaked garments, suffered terribly. Before daylight, January 1st, the mud and water which covered the earth had congealed to solid ice to the depth of over an inch. The oldest inhabitants there stated that they had never seen ice so thick before, and they verily believed that the Yankies brought down all the cold.

The Thirty-fifth had re-enlisted, and were about to start for Indiana to enjoy their brief furlough, and for several days this re-enlisting was a fruitful theme for discussion among the men of the Eighth, a good many opposing re-enlisting on account of the probability of serving under new and strange officers at the expiration of their first service. Many would say, " If we could only be sure we could keep our present officers with us after our first term, we would not care to fight this infernal rebellion until these fool Southerners will be willing to go home and become peaceable, law abiding citizens; and we kind 'o want to see the thing through, anyhow." Col. Moore, commanding the brigade, appointed the author recruiting officer for the Eighth, and in less than one week three-fourths of seven of the old companies signed re-enlistment papers, viz: Companies F, I, D, H, E, K and G. I had a laborious task filling out enlistment blanks and muster-in rolls. Several of the company commanders, on the eve of starting for home, gave all their time and attention to invoicing and turning over quartermaster stores, and arranging their vouchers preparatory to settling with the government; therefore they had no time to assist the busy recruiting officers, or any one else. The actual doubling of companies was not effected until the 25th of January, and was as follows:

Companies C and B formed Company A, Captain J. Wilson, commander.

Companies E and I formed Company B, Captain C. D. Benton, commander.

Companies H and G formed Company C, Captain Wright, commander.

Companies D and K formed Company K, Captain W. G. Smallwood, commander.

Companies A and F formed Company E. Captain Ketchins was assigned to this company, but immediatety resigned, and Lieutenant J. S. Tye took command of Company E.

The officers that were mustered out were: Captains Powell, Gunn, Martin and Dixon; Lieutenants Neal, Sail, Carson, Hughes, Blackwell, Elliott and McGuire.

Thus our regiment became the Eighth Battalion Kentucky Volunteers, infantry, numbering only four hundred and eighteen men and fourteen line officers, a major, yet in rebel prison, Quartermaster Kindred, our chaplain, Adjutant E. Park, and Sergeant-Major Mosely. Captain Benton, in Captain Wilson's absence, took command, and the evening of the 25th we received an order to march on the 26th. Fifty non-veterans of the Twenty-first Kentucky were assigned to our command, Lieutenant G. Lewis commanding.

Our mules had been hard worked and badly fed, many of them having died during this uncommon cold weather, and we could only muster eight teams. One of these the Twenty-first boys were allowed to use to carry their baggage until the return of that regiment from Kentucky. Thus we had more baggage than transportation.

Early on the 27th the Eighth moved out of their warm, snug quarters, which they had flattered themselves they would enjoy until the veteran boys would be furloughed and return. Another regiment marched in as we left, and took possession of our neat little town of cabins. Tim, our Irishman, said: "Captain, we are the boys as obaze orthers; but indade it's bad tratement to have us worrek loik nagers to build thim illigant shanties, as any dacent ommen would feel proud av, and now, bejabbers, thim lazy spalpeens are to have the good quarthers." But the men did not generally make complaint. We had endured too many sudden surprises and disappointments to make a fuss, even to leave the "illigant shanties" in mid winter. True, the veterans said, "we would much rather have started home on our promised furlough than off down in Dixie, at this time." Sergeant F. P. Wood was left in charge of our extra baggage and a few convalescents. The battalion, under command of Captain Benton, bivouacked at the "Narrows." While some of the men were playfully placing percussion caps on the railroad track for passing trains to pop, one member of Company E had his eye put out by a piece of cap.

The 28th, with the division, we halted for the night at White Sides, and the following day reached the northern base of Lookout Mountain.

The 29th the command passed through Chattanooga, and camped for the night at the foot of Mission Ridge, on a portion of the recent battle ground. The deserted rebel works, the bullet-riddled trees, with scattered shell and shot, were all that denoted it to have been the recent scene of a terrible conflict.

The 30th the division moved on up the Knoxville Railroad to Tyner's Station, and went into camp, where we remained a few days.

The 1st day of February I succeeded in mustering into the veteran service one hundred and forty-five men of the Eighth, and, by order of General Stanley, I returned to Bridgeport and collected eight of the battalion, that were in the Pioneer Corps, and returned to Ooltewah Station on the 4th, where I found the battalion.

The 5th our brigade moved on up the railroad, making short marches and keeping pace with the government employes and construction train, repairing the road as we went. The work was being pushed forward in order to reach and re-build the destroyed bridge over the Tennessee, at Charleston, our forces having destroyed it to prevent Longstreet from reinforcing Bragg during the battle at Mission Ridge.

On the evening of the 6th we halted within a mile of the pretty town of Cleveland. Colonel Walters, commanding the brigade, made his headquarters in the house of Rebel Congressman Tibbs', and the Eighth Kentucky and Thirty-first Illinois went into camp on a hill near by. If there were ever a set of men in this world gifted with thorough self-reliance, the Eighth boys were the men. It often required great fortitude to bear without murmuring the many little vexations and disappointments incident to the march and camp. We had just left good quarters, and were here on a bare, bleak hill, a cold evening, our old tents full of holes, the principal part of our cooking vessels and extra baggage far behind, but no matter where or when we halted, the Eighth boys were at home. They had learned precisely what to do first, and they did it here. Fires soon began to twinkle over the bare hill, and our old, leaky tents rose like the work of enchantment. Some had dog tents, that lay snug to the earth, like mushrooms. Soon the fragrant aroma of coffee and tortured bacon suggested creature comforts that were truly animating, under any circumstances. We all knew that the movements of regiments were as blind as fate ; none of us could tell to-night where we would be to-morrow, yet on the morning of the 7th, at the first glimmer of daylight, our camp was astir, and preparations began as if every man expected to spend the remainder of the winter here. Bricks were hauled from an old kiln of secession proclivities. Chimneys were built, and some fire places artistically plastered with the inevitable red clay, and by 10 o'clock one mess had found an old crane, on which swung a legless pot, a donation from an old darkey's kitchen ; stools and bedsteads were tumbled together by the the roughest of carpenters, and before night the interior of our rude homes began to wear a home look. Here, as elsewhere, our Kentucky boys did not long remain ignorant of the surrounding country, and its vegetable and animal productions. In less than two days they had tasted water from every spring, knocked persimmons from the best trees, milked some of the neighbors' cows, roasted pigs and picked chickens. Not a few made the acquaintance of the Cleveland girls, and knew how many were Union and how many were rebels, and how many brothers they had in the rebel army. Thus life with us began at this place.

But we did not neglect our part of the labors, throwing up a good line of rifle pits, and contributing our quota for the picket line.

The 10th of February Major Glenn, United States Paymaster, gladdened the eyes of the veterans by unloading at Captain Wright's quarters his heavy money chest. They were all paid up to the 31st of December, 1863, and received their first installment of bounty, $200 each. In a few days after Major Johnson paid off the non-veterans up to the same time. Now the veteran boys were ready, willing and impatiently waiting to be furloughed, and they expected to start soon. Said they to each other: "Old Grandpap Thomas knows what he's about. He intends for us to go home while we've plenty of money." But these calculations and fond expectations were for the present doomed to disappointment, for on the night of the 22d we received orders to march at daylight, the 23d, with only two wagons, one for rations and one for spades and picks, and only perfectly able bodied men to march. Those unable for severe duty to remain in command of a commissioned officer. This order, the boys said, certainly meant business, if not more unpleasantness with the Johnny Rebs. Some of the men that did not re-enlist, who did not expect to be furloughed, joked the veterans, tauntingly saying: "That's the kind of furloughs old Grandpap Thomas gives you—a cartridge box with sixty rounds of fresh cartridges." The veterans would reply: "Yes, you'll laugh on the other side of your mouths when we board the cars for home; it's all right, we will bide our time." Colonel Walters ordered that Captain Wright be left in charge of the camps and convalescents of the Eighth and Thirty-first Illinois.

On the morning of the 23d the officers and men, especially the veterans, left their money with me, each man's bounty and pay being enveloped with name endorsed thereon, many of them remarking that they desired that their money should find its way home to their wives or friends, if they never did. Captain Benton, in command of the Eighth, joined our old brigade at Blue Springs, and marched with the division on a reconnoissance against the enemy, near Dalton.

The 25th and 26th, skirmished with the enemy at Buzzard Roost. At times the firing was fierce. The Eighth displayed the dauntless courage for which Kentucky's sons are noted. Five of the Eighth were slightly wounded.

On the night of the 26th General Thomas ordered many fires to be made, having the men light long strings of fences, by throwing two pannels together, and making much noise, as if receiving reinforcements. This caused the enemy to fall back. Then, at the hour of midnight, our forces silently marched back, arriving at Blue Springs, six miles from Cleveland, on the 28th of February, when the writer, with the convalescents and baggage wagons, joined the battalion. The same day Captain Wilson, Quartermaster Kindred, Adjutant Park and the six furloughed men returned to the command. We remained one day at Blue Springs, trying to keep dry in our old, leaky tents.

The first day of March Captain Wilson resumed command, and at the same time we received orders from General Thomas to march immediately to the city of Chattanooga. We loaded up our camp and garrison equipage, in a heavy rain, and had a slippery, muddy, wet day's march. Arrived at Tyner's Station late in the evening, and were prospecting for a place to bivouack for the night. There being a freight train about to start for the city, Captain Wilson conceived the idea of giving us a free ride of two hours, and a cold one it was, too, for as night came on the rain ceased, the wind changed to the northwest, and blew cold and fierce. Our garments being thoroughly soaked, made our situation on the top of the boxes very unpleasant. On arriving at the depot, Captain Wilson and myself, after considerable difficulty, found General Steadman, commanding the post, and reported. The general in person conducted us to a small eminence, near to and west of Fort Wood, and informed us that here we would pitch our camp. But here was dilemma—we had nothing to pitch, not even a ration to pitch into our gnawing stomachs. Our wagons, containing all our equipage and rations, was ten miles in the rear. The wind increasing in power and cold, our clothing soon froze stiff, and thus, hungry and cold, we wore out the night hovering over some small, smoky, green wood fires. By much exertion, even more than a ten miles march, we jumped, danced and burnt our shins alternately; but as everything earthly has an end, so at last the king of day came smiling up over Mission Ridge. Some of us officers, feeling the urgent demands of the "inner man," hastened into the city on the hunt for some breakfast. The Central Hotel being the only house open (a place well and long remembered, and noted only for high prices and poor fare), we made energetic efforts to get on the outside of one dollar's worth of grub. As soon as our wagons arrived we put the men to hauling the old bricks and boards from the numerous deserted camps, and the remembrance of our bitter experience of the previous night stimulated us to a lively diligence in preparing quarters. Here we felt sure we would build our last chimney, having enjoyed the luxury of seven different winter quarters since October. The men built small board houses, using the shelter tents as a covering, each with a neat brick chimney, all laid off in regulation style. In a few days the camp of the Eighth again wore a neat and comfortable appearance.

The 5th March, Quartermaster Kindred succeeded in meeting our requisitions for new clothing, many of the men, especially the veterans, receiving entire new outfits. As they expected soon to be permitted to visit home and friends, they not only needed, but deserved, the best Uncle Samuel could furnish.

The 9th March, Captain Wilson issued his order the boys called the "chuck-a-luck order." That officer, having a strong prejudice against gambling of any description, also a wish for the best interests of the men, ordered every man arrested found playing cards, chuck-a-luck, or any other game, for money, the officer to seize the money up or "staked" and appropriate the same for the benefit of the sick of the battalion. But little money was ever found as "staked," the sporting men of the Eighth being a little too cunning for that. But General Steadman's order was to arrest all men found by the police guards gambling, and confine them in the military prison there for a specified time. Some of our Eighth boys were passing up the railroad cut to the Fifteenth Indiana regiment, and stopped a few minutes where some soldiers of another regiment were "chuck-a-lucking," when Steadman's guard pounced on them and arrested spectators and all. After much trouble we succeeded in having our innocent men released. General Steadman did not like to keep healthy, able-bodied men idle long at a time, consequently he soon had a large squad of would-be gamblers out in the valley burying the carcasses of dead horses and mules, causing no little comment by the soldiers, such as "Here's your mule."

While on picket the night of the 10th, the writer heard the following conversation between one of our sentinels and an officer of the Anderson Cavalry. The latter, after giving the countersign, passed in and said:

"What regiment is yours?"

Guard—"The Eighth Kentucky."

Officer—"Well, see here, I want this flag tale settled. Who first took the flag on Lookout the 25th November?"

Guard—"The Eighth Kentucky, you bet!"

Officer—"When I was at home in Pennsylvania I heard a fellow make a speech, and he lauded the Twenty-eighth Pennsylvania for that honorable feat. I told him and the crowd that it was the Eighth Kentucky, and I came very near having a fight on account of my statement."

Guard—"Well, captain, you was mighty right, and you kin git a thousand good witnesses to swear to it, too."

About this time Sergeant Wood, Company C, received a letter stating that his house and entire contents were destroyed by fire. His captain soon circulated a subscription list among his company, and got one hundred and fifty dollars in a few hours, which was sent to his houseless wife and children.

The 22d March put on a blustering appearance, and old Boreas let us know what he could do even down in "Dixie" by giving us eight inches of snow. The men enjoyed, or rather endured, some lively snow-ball battles. Blood flowed from a few noses, some phrenological bumps suddenly developed to immense proportions, more than one eye was discolored, and a great many were "shot in the neck." After the fight was over general good feeling, even among the lately wounded, prevailed.

The night after this snow-ball battle the long delayed and much wished for transportation order came for the Eighth veterans, with the officers of such companies as had three-fourths re-enlisted to have transportation to Lexington, Ky., consequently the 23d was quite a busy day—some of the officers inspecting and turning over old, worn-out quartermaster stores, and the men preparing rations and washing clothing.

Early the 24th, Captain Benton and Captain Wright went to the depot and made arrangements to get aboard the cars at noon. They returned and had the now exulting veterans to assemble to receive some orders about leaving their extra blankets and clothing with the non-veterans, who would remain with Captain Wilson and a few other officers. I took the opportunity to give my company the following good advice, which I am proud to record was generally heeded by all these veteran soldiers, with only a very few exceptions :

"Soldiers and comrades: We are about to start to our homes and friends, to enjoy a thirty days' furlough. Now, my desire is that every one of you shall have all the enjoyment possible to be had in one month's time, and I, your captain, who loves you all, feel it my duty to say a few words to you, not as commands, but as advice, respecting your conduct during that time ; not that I doubt that you can and will deport yourselves as become the brave men you are. Boys, I feel proud of you and the bright name you have so justly won on so many battle fields, and my intimate association with you for two and a half years, having with you endured so many privations and hardships, and saw your cheerful obedience to all legal orders, under any and all circumstances, has cemented our friendship, that I hope is second to no other fraternal feeling. Let me earnestly request that none of you, in your brief holiday, so far forget yourselves and your standing as patriotic gentlemen as to become intoxicated. Let us show our numerous friends that we can appreciate and enjoy good society in the peaceful walks of life, as well as brave the terrors and dangers of the field of battle. For this your enemies, if you have any there, will fear and respect you the more, and your friends and sweethearts love you better. And, recollect, boys, we are not free from the restraints of military discipline until we disband; until then I shall allow no absenting from the command without permission of one of your officers. Now prepare to fall into line at eleven o'clock.''

The conclusion of this advice was greeted by deafening cheers. We will now leave Captain Wilson and the non-veterans doing regular guard and garrison duty in and around Chattanooga, and, with the reader's permission, follow the veterans home and back again to the ever changing variations of the soldier's life.

CHAPTER XVI.

THE EIGHTH VETERANS ON FURLOUGH AND RETURN TO CHATTANOOGA.

The noon train for Nashville, the 24th of March, as it wound around the base of towering Lookout, bore the one hundred and sixty-two men of the Eighth, the Eighth officers, and three colored servants, Captain Benton, Captain Wright, Captain Smallwood, and Lieutenants Williams, Harklerhodes, Tye, Lewis and Pucket. It is not strange that many of us passed unnoticed the grand scenery of snow-capped mountains, for our minds were busy with cheerful thoughts of loved ones at home. Some of us had wives and children, others sweethearts and kind fathers, mothers and sisters, all of whom had been notified by mail of our expected, but delayed, coming. We arrived at the city of Nashville at noon, the 25th. A recent accident to the railroad caused us to remain at Barracks No. 2 until the morning of the 27th. At 6 o'clock we were flying northward, and arrived at Louisville at 5 p. m. We took meals and lodging at the Soldiers' Home, where the fare was superior to many hotels, and was furnished by the government free.

On the 29th we deposited our arms and equipments at the arsenal, made out furloughs for the men and officers, and made arrangements to take the Lexington train early the 30th. We had a few men in each company that had offered to re-enlist but were rejected by the examining surgeon on account of physical disability. We officers plead earnestly with Major Sidell to have these men furloughed, but he as earnestly refused, saying: "It is entirely contrary to my orders." So we were forced to leave these good, willing and obedient men, to take their thirty days' leave at Park Barracks.

On our arrival at Lexington, 3 o'clock p. m., we gave the men their furloughs, and formally disbanded, but as the majority of them desired to go the same road, 30 or 40 miles southwest, into, Madison, Estill and adjoining counties, they concluded to go the same evening to Clay's Ferry, some fifteen miles distant. The officers took early supper at the Phœnix. It was thought best that one of the officers proceed immediately to Clay's Ferry to make arrangements for supper and lodging for the men. Procuring a good horse, I proceeded to the ferry and requested Mr. Gilbert, proprietor of the one and only hotel there, to prepare supper for about one hundred men. The astonished landlord replied: "Why, Captain, that will take everything eatable on the place." I told him that these were soldiers on furlough and were perfect gentlemen, and that I would see that every man paid him, which would enable him to purchase more supplies. Very soon every member of that family were busy preparing and cooking. The clock told the small hours of the night before the last soldier arose from the table, all being lively, but not boisterous. The next morning Gilbert said to me: "Well, sir; I have seen and fed a great many soldiers during this war, but this is the first time I ever saw so many together and not had occasion to notice some ill bred behavior, and when you called last night I had no idea of receiving anything for feeding soldiers, besides, I expected my house would be ruined. They are the most genteel set of soldiers I have seen."

The men and officers, early the 1st of April, scattered to the homes of their respective families and friends, where the time passed pleasantly and rapidly with most of us, visiting friends. The many scenes of tender meetings that took place that night and the next day, between long separated husbands and wives and other dear friends, we will leave the reader to imagine. Suffice to say, every veteran tried to improve the brief holiday to the best advantage, and quite a number of them, during that balmy spring month, found time and opportunity to woo and win the hearts and hands of blushing brides, so that they could have some one with whom to leave their money. However, many of these apparently hasty marriages had been thoroughly discussed through the mails by the contracting parties for many months.

It would, no doubt, be interesting to follow some of these brave youths of the Veteran Eighth, into some of the many, happy and festive parties, as well as joyous weddings, that took place during this bright, cheerful spring month of April, in Central Kentucky, but these appear to the writer to be too much like trespassing on the private rights or the sanctity of home, and the sacred ties that bind in union two or more hearts in a sacred love, too pure and high to drag before the public gaze. So should we not hold up to the reader's view the many tender and really affecting parting scenes that took place in Estill, Madison, Jackson and a few other counties in that part of Kentucky, about the 1st of May, 1864. But we will throw the charitable mantle of silence over them, and leave the reader to draw his or her own pictures of such scenes. Ah, this returning to the war is attended with more anxious solicitude by friends, than when the new recruit first leaves the domestic circle.

The following incident was related to the author by a friend in Clark County while on furlough: Young Mrs. C., whose love for the confederacy was something like devotion gone to seed, against the wish and advice of her loyal husband, one hot day in July, 1862, continued the preparation of her flaky pies and spicy cakes, with which she declared her intention to treat Morgan's soldiers. That sultry afternoon Mrs. C. mounted her fine saddle horse (a gift from her father on her wedding day a few months before). The cumbersome basket prevented her from using her parasol as she rode, under the burning sun, over three miles of the rough country road, contemplating the pleasure she would enjoy in feasting and cheering the "southern braves." With these happy thoughts Maggie neared the long line-like cloud of white limestone dust, that rose and hung over the hot stone pike on which were passing a part of Morgan's dirty, tired and hungry troopers, who cheered the heroic little woman as she alternately waved her handkerchief, cheered for Jeff. Davis and handed out the contents of her basket to the ravenous chivalry. When the basket was empty Mrs. C. still sat on her horse by the roadside to cheer and give encouragement to the straggling rear. Many of the latter were on foot, having lost their horses in a recent skirmish on the south side of the Kentucky River. One long-haired, tall Johnnie rebel stepped up to Maggie's side. She began to lament that her cakes were all gone. He interrupted her, saying:

"Never mind, my little queen; I'm not much a-hungry, but I'm d—d tired, and I want this here hoss."

Mrs. C. replied : " O, sir ! but I am your friend; I am for southern rights."

" Wall, now, beauty, if yer sich a bully friend to the south as yer lets on to be, yer'l hev no 'bjections ter my havin' a good hoss to ride and fight Yankees on !"

Maggie remonstrated, saying she could never let "Coaly" go to war.

The parley ended by the long-armed rebel reaching up and clasping the small waist with his large hands, lifting the little, indignant, screaming woman to the ground. Depositing her saddle by her, the rebel mounted, and, with mock courtesy, bowed, saying : " Miss, this ere present does credit ter yer principles, and this ere hoss shall put in his best licks fur our cause," and galloped away.

Late that afternoon a very tired and mad little woman, with face sun-burned, her best dress and fine gaiters badly soiled, arrived home, where her anxious, loving husband stood awaiting her return. With fresh tears she sobbed out:

"O, John! I want you to get a horse and follow that rotten, thieving gang of men, and take 'Coaly' away from them."

John replied to his wife: "Now, Maggie, you have had your little romance, and I hope you are satisfied with the loss of one $300 horse. I am not fool enough to put myself to the trouble to follow your friends to give them another good horse, and probably get a cursing for my pay. No, dear, one horse and one little lesson learned will do for this time."

Mr. C. said after that day Maggie could not be persuaded to sing "In Dixie's Land I'll take my stand," but that she came over and took her stand by him for the Union, and we have no doubt smilingly approved his voting for Garfield in 1880.

The furloughed officers and our three faithful servants met the 30th at the United States Hotel, in Louisville, and reported at Park Barracks, the 1st day of May. In a few days all the men reported except a few who were sick. Private Ingram, Company D, one of the non-veterans left here, had died. On the 6th, about all our men having reported, we put on our "war harness" and boarded the evening train, and arrived at Nashville early the 7th, where we met Lieutenant C. Park and twenty of the Eighth, having in charge a number of rebel prisoners. We left Nashville at noon and were delayed at Wartrace two hours. Our boys called out our old hotel-keeper, Hailey, alias "Pig-tracks," who said he was "yit loyal," and he was given three cheers. We awoke early the 8th, at Stevenson, Ala., and all took breakfast at the new Soldiers' Home. From there to the city of Chattanooga we had a hot and unpleasant ride in the sun on top of the blistering, painted box cars. On entering our old camp we were hailed with hearty cheering. The familiar valley and surrounding mountains were now clothed in beautiful green, decked with a profusion of flowers. Our encampment also wore a neat and comfortable appearance ; and we were not at all displeased to learn that our little battalion would not move on to the front, where General Sherman had just commenced his long and bloody summer campaign, but would remain as a part of the garrison guards—not that any of the Eighth desired to shirk the sterner duties and brave new dangers, but knowing this duty had to be performed, were quite willing to remain and endure the monotony of settled soldiering, for a while at least, though our various duties were almost as constant. We could have our neat quarters to return to, where we could enjoy refreshing sleep, making a much better substitute for a home than our brave comrades could possibly have at the front. General Steadman said he had made a special request of General Thomas that he be permitted to retain the Eighth here.

Although the recently returned officers were pleased with our camp and satisfied with our prospective duties, a few of us were in a dilemma about those important appendages, the cooks. The colored boys who had returned with us to Nashville, from some cause, failed to get on the train with the soldiers at that place. At breakfast on the morning of the 10th, Captain Wright and Captain Benton were lamenting this grievance, and discussing ways and n.eans to have the absent cooks' places filled with substitutes. Just then Bristo's ebony countenance, with two rows of shining ivory, made its appearance at the open tent door. "Hello, Bristo! come in and give a report of your conduct in deserting the service." "Dat I will, Cap'n," at the same time taking off his hat and making a clownish salute. "Yer see, I neber tended to lebe yer, cap'n; it wuz you alls lef dis nigger." "Well," says Captain Benton, "but where is Simp?" "I speck he's dar wid his folks. He say to me, 'Bris, I'se found my mudder an' de odder chilen,' an' we went down dar to see em, an' we jist got de best kind o' dinner, an' I say 'Simp, dey'l lebe us, sho—let's be trablin'.' Den yer orter seed dat ole yaller 'omen! She jist cling to Simp, cryin'. At last he guv up, and say ter me: 'Bris, tell Cap'n Wright I's sorry to lebe him, but dat I'll pay him dat ten dollars ef it takes till de day ob judgment.' Den I lays roun' dat depot till last night, den I crep in a box car on de grain, an' nobody see me till dis mornin'. Whoop, doh, what a cussin' I got from de guard. I gib him half a dollar, an' he let me crawl back, an' I here, an' gwine to stay, cap'n, ef yer lets me." Bristo was duly restored to his former standing as cook for Captain Wright and his two lieutenants, without loss of pay and allowances, and remained a faithful servant until the command was discharged.

GARRISON DUTIES—SOMETHING OF THE INHABITANTS IN DIXIE.

Among our other daily duties as garrison guards of Chattanooga, an officer and from twenty to fifty men were called for every few days to guard trains to the front, or trains and prisoners to Nashville. Occasionally an officer and company would be detailed to help drive and guard a drove of beeves to the front. Probably at the same time from twenty to thirty men of the Eighth would be ordered to unload grain from the cars. Thus, it was often that we had over half of the battalion on train guard duty, making it close work to furnish our quota for pickets.

On the 18th May, Captain Smallwood and Lieutenant Tye and fifty men went to Nashville with six hundred rebel prisoners in charge. On arriving, Captain Goodwin, provost marshal, sent them on to Louisville, Ky., with the Johnnies. They returned the 23d, and again, the 31st, Captain Smallwood and fifty men made a trip to Nashville with prisoners in charge, each officer being detailed for train guard in succession as his name appeared on the roster.

But, to give a detailed account of all our various duties and expeditions as train guards, &c., would require a much larger volume than the present one, therefore we shall only be table to take up a few incidents in their regular order in the next chapter.

Our picket line on the south side of the river extended in a circuit of about six miles, from the mouth of Citico Creek above to two miles below the city. This line was divided into six different stations or reserve posts. Details from the Eighth generally picketed stations three and four. The latter extended across the Rossville road. The post commander ordered that all citizens coming to or returning from the city be admitted only at that point, those without passes to be guarded to the provost marshal, where, if Mr. or Mrs. Citizen was "all right," they obtained a pass to return through the lines. This post, therefore, required a special guard of a commissioned officer and eight men. All the surviving members of the Eighth Kentucky will doubtless remember many amusing conversations had at this Rossville Station, No. 4, with some of the droll natives of Tennessee and Upper Georgia, who frequently came fifteen or twenty miles, often on foot, to trade in the city. They were generally old men, boys and women. They usually came laden with marketable produce, which they exchanged for groceries. Some came to beg from the government, especially after the war department authorized post commissaries in certain localities to issue rations to loyal women where they had a son or husband in the United States service.

Among the many that came to Chattanooga to try Uncle Sam's generosity were really many deserving people, who were no less needy than their disloyal neighbors that often came and gave ludicrous reasons for claiming aid from the government.

The 7th June, a droll, middle-aged woman and a stout boy came up and were requested by the guard to take a seat in the shade until our escort guards returned. After wiping the perspiration from her tough-looking face with a large red "bandaner," she addressed me, saying:

"Mr. Cap'n, can one draw rations in Chatternooga neow?"

I gave her a short explanation of the order, telling her it depended altogether upon her circumstances. Her face underwent what in some countenances would have been a blush. She again brought the mammoth handkerchief into use, and demurely asked: "Well, Mr. Captain, don't you think that when the seceshers, that us critters back, eat up all our last year's crop, and then you'ens last fall just cleaned out the last sweet tater; and all this from a lone widder that's got seven children, that's got no daddy, is a sarcumstance enough." I readily admitted that if that was her marvelous condition, she certainly should be entitled to government rations, and she returned in the evening highly pleased, with all she and one of the utterly fatherless boys could carry.

Another day, soon after, I was on duty at the same station, as captain of the guard. An old lady and a boy drove up in a little, rickety old wagon, drawn by a little black scrub ox, very little larger than a good Southdown sheep. The harness was a single yoke, into which the shafts were secured by wooden pins, and a hemp rope around the ox's stubby horns. As they halted, one of the guards remarked: "Well, that rig beats anything I've seen in Dixie." The old lady, with considerable spirit, replied: "O, sir, if it's Buck and the wagon you calls a rig, I can tell you it's so much better'n lots of our neighbors can do, I kinder feel proud, for it's a sight easier'n walking." On the arrival of this primitive conveyance at Captain Davis' office he politely requested the occupants to remain seated in the wagon a few minutes, and that smiling official hurried into an artist's tent, near by. Very soon the artist was out on the pavement, adjusting his camera. The old lady discovered his maneuvers, and instantly began to scream and make frantic efforts to leave the wagon, saying, " O, for the good Lord's sake, don't kill we'uns."

The captain, after assuring her that no harm should be done, that they only wished to take her picture, and explaining to her the use of the camera, she exclaimed: "Well, 'pon my soul and body, and that's what you'ens makes pictures with. I made sure it was some kind of a Yankee gun; it did look so frightful with that are man a taken sight at me and Johnny. I tell you, I thought our time had come, sure." That evening, as she passed out of the lines, the old lady appeared to take great pleasure in showing us her picture, saying, "See, there's me a holding the basket of berries, and there's Johnny, the wagon, and old Buck, too; all jest looking natural as life, and all done most as quick as shootn', only I didn't hear anything pop; but I tell you, Mr. Captain, I was scart." We offered five dollars for that picture, but it was evidently not for sale. The country people generally came with their marketables to the city on Saturdays in great numbers, which compelled our guards to economize time and travel by escorting citizens to the city in squads of a dozen or twenty. The 14th of June, just after the guard had left with one of these squads, there came to the post two delicate, fair haired girls, the eldest probably sixteen and the younger about thirteen years of age, accompanied by an old negro, who bore on her head a large basket of huckleberries. The girls each had a peck basket of this early fruit. They took seats in the shade of our tall hedge fence, to await the return of my guards. In these young ladies' manners and speech I noticed a degree of refinement above the ordinary people. Their dresses, though somewhat worn and faded, were neat fitting and scrupulously clean. I felt interested to know something of their peculiar misfortune, feeling certain that they had seen better and happier days. In compliance to my inquiries, the oldest girl gave a short statement, in substance, as follows:

At the commencement of the war their father owned one of the best plantations on Chickamauga

River, and worked about fifty slaves. Their two brothers had early joined the rebel ranks, and one of them fell in battle in 1861. The father died from disease in 1862, leaving their mother, and with a faithful old negro man as boss of the slaves, they got on very well, until the great battle of Chickamauga. On Sunday the contending armies drew near in furious conflict. The mother, two daughters and the old black woman, for safety, took refuge in the cellar; but soon a wicked shell exploded in and set fire to their fine house. They then fled to the woods, in the rear of the rebel line, and found shelter in the cabin of a poor white woman, whose husband was also a rebel soldier. The loss of property, excitement, and over exertion, proved too much for the feeble mother, who, after a few weeks illness, died. The slaves all left the houseless and fenceless plantation, and they were still sharing the humble shelter and coarse, scant fare of the war widow and her children. The kind-hearted old colored woman yet remained true to them, and they had just learned that their only brother was a prisoner in Chattanooga. He had taken the oath of allegiance, but would be sent north of the Ohio River, and they desired to see him before he left.

While she related this sad story, vainly trying to keep back the unbidden tears, our hearts ached in sympathy for these tender girls, reared in a home of luxurious comfort, now homeless and nearly friendless orphans, toiling with tender hands to gather wild berries and bearing them over ten miles of hot, dusty roads, that they might help buy a few necessaries of life. The old darkey, with tears in her eyes, said: "Dar, Miss Lilly, don't cry befo' de boss, fur I'se gwine to stick to yo', chile, so I is."

The next day, after being relieved, I stated to Adjutant General Moe briefly the case of the rebel prisoner and brother. Before night he was employed by the chief of transportation, at Chattanooga, to work in the depot rubbing up locomotives, and his two sisters found friends in the city, with whom they boarded at the expense of the ex-rebel.

CHAPTER XVII.

The 22d June, 1864, by order of General Steadman, I took command of a guard of forty men—twenty of the Eighth and twenty of the Sixty-eighth Indiana—to guard 370 federal prisoners to the front. They were deserters and bounty jumpers belonging to various commands, gathered up principally from the large cities, and were as dirty, lousy and reckless a set of men as could well have been found on the globe. Some of them boasted that they had received six bounties. At noon I received the rolls and prisoners, and, with my guards, boarded the top of two long freight trains containing ammunition. The power of the unobstructed rays of the sun on the newly painted boxes was oppressive, and the water in our canteens soon became a few degrees above blood heat. As the rebels were daily tearing up rails, placing torpedoes between the ties, and frequently cutting the telegraph wires and firing on passing trains from the brush, we made short halts at all the stations to telegraph front and back. A train had been blown up, near Resaca, the evening before, by a torpedo, evidently the work of disloyal citizens, or emissaries harbored by them. The thought of riding over tons of powder and striking one of these explosive and inflammable magazines was yet more unpleasant than the fear of rebel bullets or the blistering heat. At dark we arrived at Resaca, and were telegraphed to lay over until morning. We passed a sleepless night. Some of our "jail birds" were evidently anxious to give us the slip, but the untiring vigilance of the guards, aided by the light of a bright, full moon, enabled us to keep our prisoners within prescribed limits, but not until several of them had been touched by the persuasive point of the bayonet. Early the 23d I made requisition on Colonel Moore, commanding the post, and received one day's scant rations, which the bounty jumpers ate for breakfast. At Kingston we met two long trains of hospital cars filled with recently wounded men. The floors were paved with bleeding heroes of the Fourth Corps. I found Colonel Price, Lieutenants Brown and Buckley, of the Twenty-first Kentucky, and many others whose faces were familiar, among the wounded. How our hearts warmed toward these brave men who had stood by us so nobly at Stone River, Chickamauga, Lookout and other places. Looking through the train for acquaintances, white, ghostly bandages, with here and there a large rusty spot of blood, met our gaze on every side. As the attendants came along with canteens of stimulating coffee, graced only with sugar, tin cups were extended in all sorts of hands except strong ones. The dull, pale faces brightened as the cups were filled, and the ghost of a cheer greeted the coffee man as he entered another car. Standing over Lieutenant Brown, I asked him how he was. He looked up, with a faint smile, and replied: "Why, captain, bully!" Common as was this army phrase, it sounded from the pale lips of Brown, who was badly wounded, manly and noble. These and two more car loads were wounded in action the 22d at Kulp's House, near Pine Mountain. We did not reach Big Shanty until near dark. This was the terminus of our railroad travel. After deploying my guards around the prisoners I went to General Sherman's headquarters, in a house near the station. The adjutant general readily consented to furnish me guides to pilot us to the headquarters of General Thomas, where I was ordered to report. At that moment the great "flanking" general came walking in, his heavy sword and spurs clanking over the bare floor. The adjutant addressed him, saying, "General, here is a captain from Chattanooga, with a lot of bounty jumpers and scalawags from our army. I have just sent for one of the boys to pilot him to Thomas' headquarters." The general stood meditatively about one minute, then said to me: "Captain, the road is through swamps and thickets, full of stubs and mud holes, and it is cloudy. You had best form a bull-pen of your guards around your pets and wait until morning, then you shall have an escort." I thanked the tall old hero, and corralled the prisoners for the night. The 24th, our six miles' march was slow, many of the prisoners being barefooted and quite lazy. At 10 o'clock, a. m., I turned over to Colonel Parkhurst, provost marshal, Department of the Cumberland, our pets. His adjutant proceeded to call the roll and pick out the men that belonged to that department. The skirmishers near the base of Kenesaw Mountain kept up an incessant popping during the evening, while the cannon of the enemy thundered from their high position east and south of us. At 2 o'clock, p. m., we again took charge of our pets, except the 130 belonging to that department, and proceeded eastward, in the rear of the long lines of our vigilant army, to the head quarters of General McPherson, Department of the Tennessee, situated nearly north of, and near the base of Kenesaw. Here Colonel Wilson, provost marshal, was kind enough to relieve my guards during the night, but said he could not furnish us rations. I then called on General McPherson, who, after hearing the statement of the supperless condition of both guards and prisoners, and the sleepless vigilance that had been required to watch these men, most of whom dreaded the idea of a court marshal, or worse, digging picket holes under fire, approved my requisition, and soon a wagon was dispatched to Big Shanty, and returned about midnight with the much needed grub. The moonlight enabled the pickets to keep up a lively skirmish the latter part of the night, along the side of the mountain. But the loss of sleep for two nights enabled us to sleep regardless of hostilities within artillery range of Adjutant F. Earl's tent, where we reposed.

On calling the roll, the 25th, we found eighty-eight of our charge belonged to the Tennessee, and in accordance with Sherman's order, we took charge of the remaining prisoners and started to General Scofield's, Department of the Ohio, on the extreme right wing. Feeling refreshed, we retraced our steps westward, but soon discovered all the right wing of the army on another flank movement to the right, and it was 4 p. m. before we came up with General Thomas and staff, bivouacked. Colonel Parkhurst sent his provost guards on to Scofield's headquarters with their prisoners, and again we had short relief from the bounty jumpers. But early the 26th the provost guards returned to us ninety-eight of our scallawags, that evidently belonged to the Army of the Potomac. At the same time we took charge of one hundred rebel prisoners, some of them captured the evening before. One of them intimated to me that he should take the oath to Uncle Sam, and quit the South forever. Said he: "I'll tell yer ef we couldn't stop your army from flanking us at Resaca or Altoona, 'taint no use to try it south of Kenesaw, and that 'll be abandoned before to-morrow." I asked him how he knew. "Well, yesterday mornin' we had orders to keep everything packed up, ready for a move, and we've heard that order so often we all know d—d well it means retreat." Arriving at Big Shanty at 1 p. m, we cooped our prisoners in empty box cars and arrived in Chattanooga at midnight of the 27th. Escorted our prisoners to a large church, during a heavy rain and thunder storm, and were relieved, wet and hungry. Some of the Eighth boys remarked: "Train guard duty aint no durned soft thing, after all.

About the 1st of July our senior surgeon, John Mills, was assigned the position of medical director of the large field hospital on Cameron Hill, several hundred recently wounded patients having arrived from the front, who were wounded in Sherman's unsuccessful assault on Kenesaw Mountain.

All the garrison at Chattanooga were up at arms on the morning of the Fourth of July, General Pillow, with a force of the enemy, having been reported near Lafayette.

The 4th, as the sun arose over Mission Ridge, in accordance with General Steadman's order, at the signal gun, a 100 pounder, every steam whistle of locomotives, steamboats and shops about the city, simultaneously, rent the still morning air with a roaring, screeching sound, more unearthly than the writer ever expected to hear. Nine salutes and screams were repeated at noon and sunset, making the mountain-walled valley echo, as I then thought and hoped, the death knell of the confederacy and rebellion. The day was celebrated by some officers, soldiers and loyal citizens, by a pic-nic and dancing fandango at Lookout Mountain. From the picket station I viewed the pleasure seekers with a field glass, joyous groups of shoulder-strapped and blue-coated men, and country maids, tripping their light feet in unison with the lively music, contrasted with the hostile scenes enacted on the same grounds seven months previous, when our boys treated the frowning rebels with cold lead, and now their smiling sisters to expensive ice cold lemonade.

About this time General Steadman issued orders that all male citizens, living between Chattanooga and Dalton, within three miles of the railroad, should come in and establish their loyalty, or be compelled to leave the country. This seemingly harsh order was caused by the frequent obstructions found placed on the railroad track, and believed by the general to have been done by citizens, or those harbored by them. These sweeping orders caused the now excited country people to flock into the city by scores. One very hot day in July, our picket guards escorted to headquarters over two hundred. Many of these once slave owning aristocrats, whose love for the "divine institution" of the South and hatred for Yankees had kept them from the city for many months, now came smiling up to the picket line, their fair daughters availing themselves of this rare opportunity to once more come to the city to do a little shopping, though truth compels me to say that the majority of them came on foot. The reader must remember that even the wealthy farmers here had, by the urgent demands for horses for the waning confederacy, been left without even the proverbial army mule. At the picket station, these would-be aristocratic ladies usually halted under our friendly shade to cool, shake off the dust, and rest. Many were the sighs and wishes made by them for the return of the good, old happy days, before the war, when they could ride in the old family carriage, with the dressed up darkey driver perched on top. But alas, for rebellion's folly, the days of slavery had been numbered, and the mere chattel would come out of all this blood, carnage, and suffering of many innocent people, a man with so called equal rights. But few citizens from the country, and seventy from the city, were ordered north.

On the 18th of July, while a few of the Eighth guards were passing some women and a wagon load of produce into town, some of the Third Wisconsin Battery boys stopped the wagon and began to help themselves. E. Sparks clubbed his gun and knocked two of the battery boys down. Some demonstrations of hostility caused the Eighth boys to cock their pieces, while the sergeant informed them they would shoot the first man that came within three feet of the wagon. After considerable blustering and threats by the Third, they retired, and after that the 8th boys had no trouble with them robbing wagons.

Chaplain Kindred, like the faithful soldier, kept watch to thwart, if possible, the enemy, or enemies, of the soul, for there were many, had our regular Sunday sermon, also prayer meeting, and preaching occasionally in the evening. Frequently a preaching brother of the Military Christian Commission called and gave us a sermon. To one unacquainted with camp life it would have been a novel, if not an impressive sight, to see on a beautiful moonlight night, at the sound of singing, by a squad of soldiers, some old familiar hymn, the brawny, sun-tanned veterans, each with his camp stool in hand, gathering around the singers in the space between the tents, where the sermon would be respectfully listened to by all with as much decorum as in our churches at home.

The 18th of July Captain Benton was appointed assistant post inspector, thus leaving us one officer less for daily duty.

The 22d we were rejoiced at the prospect of the fall of Atlanta; but this news was soon followed with the sad tidings of the death of Gen. McPherson, and for a few days our wounded came back on the cars in fearful numbers; also, a good many rebel prisoners, whom our command guarded on trains as far north as Nashville. The Fifty-first Indiana Infantry composed part of our garrison, after the Fifteenth Indiana were mustered out, in May.

Colonel Streight, of Libby Tunnel notoriety, joined his regiment, the Fifty-first Indiana, the 20th.

About the 1st of August all our non-veterans that had been assigned to the pioneer corps, returned with Lieutenant W. Park to the command.

Politics began to be a theme of general discussion with the soldiers, many earnestly desiring now to free the negro, but bitterly opposed allowing him all the rights of a white citizen.

The 14th of August we were aroused from the lethargy of our monotonous picket duty, by the rebels making a raid on Dalton, Georgia, and threatening other points nearer. The now terrified Union citizens came flocking into our lines for protection. Gen. Steadman, with the Sixty-eighth, Fifty-first and Twenty-ninth Indiana, and one regiment of colored troops (the Fourteenth), and several pieces of the Wisconsin Battery, hastened out on the train to the rescue, the remainder of the colored brigade here supplying the place of the Hoosier boys on picket. This being the first time the Eighth boys had done duty with the darkeys, caused some grumbling at being left behind, when there was a chance, as the boys said, of helping put down the rebellion. But like good soldiers, they did their duty, and only laughed at their novel situation, saying: "We'll do anything honorable to cripple the enemy."

Late on the 15th, General Steadman and the four regiments returned, having routed Wheeler's gang. The Indiana boys gave us a good report of the colored regiment, who made a gallant charge, coming to close quarters with the enemy, and in several instances refused to show quarter, but clubbed their guns and shouted their watchword, "Remember Fort Pillow," and actually beat the brains out of several rebels offering to surrender.

Again, the 17th of August, General Steadman was telegraphed that about 2,000 rebels had appeared at Grayer's Station, north of Ringgold, and our garrison was reduced so much, and the reports of threatened attack put us all the *qui vive*. At sunset the Eighth occupied Fort Wood, and lay behind their loaded guns, "a little anxious for a brush," as the boys said, for we felt confident with our fourteen pieces, twelve pound Parrots. The other troops here also occupied the other forts; but no enemy appeared, and at sunrise we returned to our quarters, to endure one of the hottest days of the season. The power of the sun's unobstructed rays upon our thin tents, without the slightest perceptible breeze for hours, made the camp almost unendurable. At the close of this terrible, still, hot day, the white capped clouds slowly loomed up in the western horizon, from which played the zigzag streaks of lightning. The camp was unusually quiet. I lay with the walls of my tent hoisted, trying to get every breath of fresh air. I watched the gathering storm. The thunder's hoarse roar, and the continuous vivid flashes of lightning, playing around the crown of grand old Lookout Mountain, appeared as if nature, in her angry mood, was trying to mimic the sad, historic scenes enacted there one last November's night, i. e., "the battle above the clouds." The nearer approach of the coming storm caused me to cease my fanciful reverie, and assist Bristo tighten down the tent pins. At 8 o'clock, while the terrific storm was raging in majestic fury, sitting on my camp stool, I suddenly found myself lying on my back, with a tingling, numb sensation through my body. In one corner of the tent knelt Bristo, praying, if not with the spirit and understanding, with lusty utterance, like, "Oh Hebenly Master, I knows I's a bad nigger; de good Lord have mussy on us, fur oh, mars cap'ns dead and, oh my shin—" I interrupted his devotional theme by asking, " Bris, are you hurt?" "De lor bress yer, cap'n, I thot you's dead, an' I skin my shin agin dat pole." At that time I heard some one in camp shout: "Abe's dead." When the storm had abated a little I learned that the lightning had struck the top pole of Company A's first tent, following down a musket, hanging bayonet downward, near the bunk of Abe Henderson, melting off the point of the bayonet and paralyzing Henderson to such a degree that he was unable to move, and not did recover his speech for several days. On the evening of the 24th of August Chaplain Burkett gave us a call, and preached one of his able sermons. I did not get to see the good old man, being sick. I lay in my tent, and had the pleasure of hearing him. From the 25th of August to the 12th of September the writer was unable to make any notes of events in the battalion, being confined to his bed at a private residence in the city.

The Democratic-Conservative-Peace party met in a national convention on the 29th August, passed a series of resolutions, and then nominated General George B. McClellan for president and George H. Pendleton for vice president. When I returned to camp the 12th September the soldiers appeared to be taking much interest in politics, having now, by an act of the Kentucky Legislature, a right to vote at our respective camps. The following resolution of the Chicago convention was a source of much comment and frequent warm discussions between those who expressed their opinions favorable to the peace party and the "Lincoln boys," who then appeared to be about half of the command:

Resolved, That this convention does explicitly declare, as the sense of the American people, that, after four years of failure to restore the Union by the experiment of war, under the pretense of a military necessity or war power higher than the constitution, the constitution itself has been disregarded in every part, and public liberty and private right alike trodden down, and the prosperity of the country impaired. Justice, humanity, liberty and the public welfare demand that immediate efforts be made for a cessation of hostilities, with a view to a convention of the states, or other peaceable means, that at the earliest practicable moment peace may be restored on a basis of the union of the states.

This was the first instance in the history of the nation in which one of the two great political parties composing the voting population had avowed its hostility in such bitter terms, not only to the existing administration, but to the conflict in which it was engaged for the maintenance of the nation's life, and had the party gone before the people with this platform, pure and simple, as the only issue between them and the party of the Union, they would have been buried so deep in scorn and contempt of the nation they would never have found a resurrection. Their chief candidate, however, who was yet quite popular with the soldiers, accepted the nomination, but repudiated the resolutions, especially those that demanded an immediate cessation of hostilities.

The following short dialogue between one of the men of Company A and Sergeant Campbell, Company C, will give the reader some idea of the interest the boys took in the coming election:

Company A—"I am still for my government, but as for my part I'll support 'Little Mac,' for if we re-elect 'Old Abe' the nigger will not only be free to take arms, but the ballot too, and I'll be d—d if I like the idea of voting by the side of a cucumber-shinned nigger; and you know there are thousands of good soldiers and loyal men at home who will support as good a conservative as McClellan."

Sergeant—"I readily admit that your party embraces many good Union men, but it embraces every secessionist, bushwhacker, guerrilla and rebel now in Kentucky, and these really recognized Union men are to screen from the world's view the disloyal hosts that are huzzaing for Mac. When you hear a fellow spouting about the d—d abolitionists having got up this war, you may set him down as a traitor or a copperhead, and they belong to the very meanest class of reptiles that crawl ; and I believe, if the case could be fully investigated, we should find that it was one of them that betrayed old Mother Eve in the Garden of Eden. Away with your nonsense about conservatism ! Do you think our noble constitution has no innate power to maintain itself that copperheads must become its conservators ? If you cast your vote for conservatism you will be spending your influence in the conservation of this hellish rebellion. We want no more men to manage public affairs who are so desperately afraid of hurting slavery. We want no more men covering half his face with his country's flag and half with the traitor's flag of rebeldom. I tell you it is all a delusion. After the horrible record of the last three years, slavery is gone. To revive or restore it you may as well call the bodies of the unnumbered dead of this war to come from their graves as to try to infuse life into the dead corpse of American slavery. This is not fanaticism, but the sober, solemn truth, and the sooner we old soldiers realize it, and conform our conduct in accordance, the better, for the sooner our army realizes this fact, the sooner will the final exterminating blow be given to this accursed, disgraceful rebellion."

The 4th September, 1864, all the troops around Chattanooga rejoiced at the news of the fall of Atlanta, nor were our feelings of joy the less on the 6th, at the news of the death of John Morgan, the guerrilla chief, who was shot in trying to escape from some of General Gillem's men, in a garden at Greenville, Tenn. Some of the Eighth boys remarked:

> Johnny rides on his raids no more,
> And ladies can wear jewelry as before.

About this time quite a number of our battalion were sick, principally from fever. Alvin Schull, Company A, a fine, promising young man, died in October, much loved and lamented by his comrades. His father, Dr. Schull, of Irvine, Ky., arrived a few days before, and conveyed his remains home.

During our long stay at Chattanooga, Chaplain Kindred held religious worship regularly in camp twice a week. Some times we had a sermon from a member of the Christian Commission, and several times were interested by the able old refugee, Chaplain Burkett, of the Twenty-first Kentucky. A marked improvement was noticed by the writer and others in the general morals, speech and conduct of the Eighth within the last year. We heard much less profanity in camp than formerly. Many had become disgusted at so much vulgar profanity and quit the habit. Others, whose convictions were deeper seated, had joined our Christian League, instituted in the Eighth and Twenty-first Kentucky in September, 1863. Doubtless many good men, now exemplary Christians, can date their start in a genuine reformation in life to some of those interesting meetings held in camp. At least the author is certain that several men have since then made such statements, their manner of life being proof of the same.

Our comparatively peaceful routine duty at Chattanooga was interrupted the 26th September. The rebel General Forrest crossed the Tennessee River at Harpeth Shoals, and made an attack on the garrison at Athens, Ala., thus threatening our long "cracker line," the N. & C. Railroad. At 4 o'clock that evening all of the Eighth able for duty marched to the depot, each man with sixty rounds of ammunition and three days' rations, leaving a few convalescents with our camp and equipage. We, in company with the Sixty-eighth Indiana, on board a train of platform cars, halted at Bridgeport and took on a good supply of axes, spades and picks. The night being very dark, the train ran slow, and reached the mouth of the Cumberland tunnel at daylight the 27th. After a hasty breakfast we laid off a line of earthworks and worked faithfully all day. We cut trees and rolled logs and large stones into line, against which the hard earth was piled breast high. At 5 o'clock, p. m., our pickets were called in, we being ordered by General Millroy to mount the first train north and proceed to Elk River bridge. After waiting in the rain until after 9 o'clock, p. m., we left the Sixty-eighth Indiana here. We halted at

Decherd to throw off our tools, and soon landed at the bridge. Lieutenant-Colonel Mayhew and three companies occupied the fort, Company C, Captain Wright, the block-house on the south side, and Lieutenant Tye and Company B that on the north. As soon as daylight appeared everybody about the fort and block-houses was at work. Water tanks were cleaned out and refilled, and every necessary preparation made to stand a protracted attack, which we had good reason to believe the rebel raiders would make that day or night. Within these bomb-proof block-houses, every man with plenty of ammunition lying at his port-hole, while the boys at the strong little fort, with its four ominous looking twelve-pounders, we felt rather anxious to have the enemy attack us, as the men said, "Probably it will be our last fight, and we intend to make it a good one." During the early part of the night a part of the enemy had crossed the railroad within a few miles and cut the telegraph. We grew more impatient waiting to hear the signal fire of our pickets. At 1 o'clock, a. m., we heard the unmistakable trample of cavalry. Then followed the discharge of several pieces of musketry in quick succession, then all was quiet, except some loud talking on picket. The Fifth Tennessee Federal Cavalry had accidentally, in their co-operative movements, run into our line. Fortunately, no harm resulted beyond the wounding of one horse. Explanations were soon made, and our Tennessee friends passed on. We were kept on the *qui vive* for several days, but had no chance to try our guns at rebels through port-holes. General Rousseau, on the 29th, gave Forrest's raiders a complete drubbing at Athens, Ala., and sent them off southwest again.

CHAPTER XVIII.

We remained at Elk River until the 20th of October, occupying the positions named in the preceeding chapter, except on the 5th, Lieutenant Williams and twenty men, of Companies H and B, were stationed at a stockade and water tank, one mile north of the bridge. We drew rations for the battalion from Tullahoma. The first five days' supply were spoiled—old moldy crackers and meat, totally unfit for human food. Colonel Mayhew ordered a board of survey, that soon reported b̄⁻ ·k to the commissary at Tullahoma, with the ⸺ ⸺u grub. During this unavoidable delay, for two days our men were forced to resort to the poorly cultivated late corn fields for bread. Some gathered unripe pumpkins, others found a few potatoes and late green beans. But as soon as rations were received the men generously made full restitution to those from whom they had been compelled to take. Our men, generally, exhibited more sympathy with families in needy circumstances in the South, than was usually shown by troops from the northern states. Though all the able bodied males were in arms against us and their country, we considered it wrong to take from helpless women and innocent children their scanty means of subsistence. We here found even those who had good farms, hard run for bare necessaries; therefore we forbid any foraging. Still the men were allowed to trade for or exchange sugar, coffee, etc., for sweet potatoes and other vegetables.

Captain Wilson returned to Chattanooga, with an order from General Millroy to bring up our camp equipage, as we had no cooking vessels. But the post commander, being equal in rank, refused to let the Eighth and Sixty-eighth Indiana camps be moved, and all the men and officers found much difficulty in cooking rations. Captain Smallwood, Lieutenant Jones and myself furnished goverment rations for a Mrs. Garner, living near the fort, and had her prepare our grub. The fine weather, light duty, and prospects of the early end of the war, made the command cheerful, under all circumstances.

The 11th, a squad of Company H, with Captain Smallwood and myself, by request of old Mr. Emery, a citizen, attended the funeral and assisted in burying his daughter, the bride of Sergeant Garland, Second Kentucky Battery, who had died suddenly two weeks after her marriage. The scarcity of able bodied citizens in the neighborhood made our assistance a matter of necessity. Without our aid the burial would have been a laborious task for the few old men and little boys. The beautiful corpse and impressive service by an army chaplain, the grief stricken husband, the moaning parents and sisters, made it indeed a solemn scene.

That evening the men's knapsacks were thrown off a train in a heap, near the fort. There was some confusion, each trying to be first to secure his indi-

sent south with a drove of beeves. We were relieved from picket duty occasionally by the Fourteenth U. S. colored regiment, and notwithstanding they were commanded by intelligent gentlemen (white officers), a few of our McClellan boys held the dusky boys in blue to be rather a disgrace to our uniform, and they thought it a hardship to be compelled to comply with the usual military etiquette and regulations, when being relieved, to make the usual salute by presenting arms, as the new guard marched past to take their position. But they consoled themselves with the thoughts of the waning fortunes of the confederacy, and their soon being again free men in a free country.

The last days of October, the Fourth Corps, under General Stanley, arrived at Chattanooga. General Sherman's famous Atlanta citizens' order was being carried out. Hundreds were daily passing north, the overtasked rolling stock on the N. & C. road being unable to transport them. Many of them had to lay over here in the depot buildings.

November 3d we were ordered by General Steadman to go to Resaca, Georgia, to relieve the garrison there, to be absent one week. Now we had concluded, as our time would be up the 15th, the General should have sent some other regiment, and to comply with this unexpected order was even more unpleasant than remaining here and picketing with the darkeys. Colonel Mayhew sent the author to the adjutant general, with a request that one officer from each company of the Eighth be allowed to stay in our camp to prepare rolls and discharge papers. The request was granted, and five officers, including the author, remained with a few men not able for duty.

The battalion went on the cars, the 3d, to Resaca, and part of the command remained there, and the balance at Calhoun, as garrison guards, until the 13th of November.

The cold, rainy season had caused us to again hover around our rudely-constructed fireplaces, and we officers were for several days quite busy with our muster-out rolls, as we expected the battalion back the 10th. But that and several days passed and we were anxiously expecting them.

The 13th being Sunday, and camp appearing unusually dull, I took a walk in the city and called on the good lady that had nursed me so kindly during my illness in September. After partaking of a good dinner, a few of us took a walk about the depot, where hundreds of families were waiting transportation north. General Sherman had decided to make the city of Atlanta strictly a military post, and in September had ordered all families in Atlanta having male representatives in the rebel lines to be sent immediately through the lines to their friends, and all other non-combatants in Atlanta to be transported north. The large depot buildings were full, and many families had provided themselves rude shelter by stretching up quilts and blankets, tent-fly fashion. Many of these people bore unmistakable evidences of refinement. Viewed under surrounding circumstances in which they were now placed, more wretched than soldier life, little or no shelter, hovering around small smoky fires, on which women were trying to cook some fat pork and boil coffee that had been given them by Uncle Sam, crying and fretting children clinging to not overly clean dress skirts, these southern women certainly did not present an amiable appearance. I could but pity these innocent women and tender children whom the sad circumstances of this useless and foolish rebellion had caused to be houseless and homeless, most of them unwilling emigrants. I could only say, God pity them! and return to my quarters pondering on the cruelties of war.

Late on the night of the 14th our pleasant dreams of home were broken by the old familiar cheering of the Eighth returning. The 15th and 16th were busy days with the officers. The evening of the latter the men were paraded and stacked arms. Ordnance, camp and garrison stores were piled, inspected, invoiced, and finally turned over to the post inspector, with proper vouchers. We slept as soundly as if no war was devastating our once happy country.

The 17th all the Eighth except Lieutenant Pucket and the veterans marched to the tent of Lieutenant Stansbury, mustering officer U. S. A., and were duly mustered out, the company officers retaining the men's discharge papers until we should reach Louisville, Ky., where we were to receive our pay.

The 18th we bid Pucket and our veteran brothers farewell, and were soon on board the cars for home.

We arrived at Nashville, where we were compelled to remain until morning. The 19th, after seeing our baggage safely housed at the Louisville depot, the officers put up at the N—— House. Much good feeling was manifested among us, some of the younger officers vieing with each other in conviviality, while a few of us older ones, who made less demonstrations of gayety, felt no less happy at the prospect of soon being once more free from military orders, and at home with our dear wives and other friends that were anxiously expecting our return.

Early the 23d day of November, 1864, the non-veterans of the Eighth assembled and formed in line our last time, marched to the United States Depository in Louisville, and all, except the officers whose accountability for government stores had not been settled, received final payment, and the men's discharge papers were by the company officers given them. Then followed a general farewell handshaking, with many earnest vows of eternal friendship, and we hastened to our respective homes, feeling confident that in a few weeks, or months at most, the cruel war would be over by the complete overthrow of the would-be Southern Confederacy.

CHAPTER XIX.

COMPANY ROSTER OF CONSOLIDATED COMPANY C, EIGHTH BATTALION KENTUCKY VOLUNTEER INFANTRY (FORMERLY COMPANIES G AND H, EIGHTH REGIMENT KENTUCKY VOLUNTEERS).

NAMES PRESENT AT MUSTER OUT, NOVEMBER 18, 1864.

Captain T. J. Wright . . . . Aged 35
First Lieutenant James R. Williams . . . . " 26
Second Lieutenant George W. Lewis . . . . " 24
First Sergeant Daniel Campbell . . . . " 41
Fourth Sergeant William T. Fielder . . . . " 21
Fifth Sergeant John F. Clemmons . . . . " 21
Wagoner, William Pitcher . . . . " 28

PRIVATES.	AGE	PRIVATES.	AGE
1 Abney, Colby	36	17 King, Francis	23
2 Aldrich, William	30	18 King, John	27
3 Bailey, Alford	39	19 Laneheart, Sidney Q.	22
4 Dennis, Pleasant	35	20 Lewis, Joseph W.	26
5 Elliott, Philip J.	22	21 Moreland, Richard	26
6 Fritz, Michael	29	22 Moore, William P.	35
7 Gibson, Hughy	25	23 Rice, John Q.	31
8 Gabbard, Greenbury	25	24 Shackleford, Maundrel E	22
9 Hurley, Gilbert	21	25 Stamper, William B.	22
10 Hornsby, William	33	26 Stamper, Marcus D.	21
11 Hall, Martin B.	28	27 Stephens, Richard	27
12 Harris, William	22	28 Tolson, Isaac	23
13 Howard, Francis	21	29 Turner, Edward	25
14 Hendricks, Elijah	35	30 Whisman, Hiram	22
15 Jones, Nathaniel	23	31 Wade, George W.	44
16 Jenkins, Parson	27	32 Webb, Elisha	29

TRANSFERRED.

Sergeant James M. Kindred, to staff, March, 1862.
Sergeant Henry Morris, to hospital steward, May, 1862.
Private Hiram Burris, to marine brigade, April, 1863.
Corporal Joshua Bingham, to invalid corps, November, 1863.
Corporal Sampson Patton, to invalid corps, November, 1863.

APPENDIX. 279

PRISONERS OF WAR.

1 Blevins, Eli A 27
2 Barnett, James A 33
3 King, Moses H 21
4 Morris, William 21

DISCHARGED.

	CAUSE.	DATE.
Captain Rhodes Winbourn. .	Physical Disability	March, 1863
Lieut. Winfield S. Spencer. .	Physical Disability	Febr'y, 1862
Lieut. Caleb S. Hughes . . .	Consolidation . .	Janu'y, 1864
Private Joseph P. Wright . .	Physical Disability	March, 1862
Private William Pucket . . .	Physical Disability	March, 1862
Corporal Francis M. Wilson .	Physical Disability	April, 1862
Private Dillard Bush	Physical Disability	May, 1862
Private John Lunsford. . . .	Physical Disability	May, 1862
Private William Baker. . . .	Physical Disability	May, 1862
Private Jeremiah Sparks. . .	Surgeon's Cert. .	May, 1862
Sergeant Robert Bingham . .	Surgeon's Cert. .	May, 1862
Private Jonathan N. Bishop .	Surgeon's Cert. .	June, 1862
Private John Groves.	Surgeon's Cert. .	June, 1862
Private Alford Blevins . . .	Surgeon's Cert. .	Sept'r, 1862
Private Jackson Moore . . .	Surgeon's Cert. .	Sept'r, 1862
Private Robert M. Marshall .	Surgeon's Cert. .	Oct'r, 1862
Private John Derbin.	Surgeon's Cert. .	Oct'r, 1862
Musician Martin V. Hall . .	Surgeon's Cert. .	Oct'r, 1862
Corporal Shipton Stephens. .	Surgeon's Cert. .	Oct'r, 1862
Private Joseph Derbin. . . .	Accidental Wound	Dec'r, 1862
Private Joseph McPherson .	Physical Disability	Dec'r, 1862
Corporal James Dixon. . . .	Surgeon's Cert. .	Janu'y, 1863
Private Francis M. Schoolcraft	Surgeon's Cert. .	Janu'y, 1863
Private Isaac Whitaker . . .	Surgeon's Cert. .	Janu'y, 1863
Private Henry Gentry. . . .	Wounds.	Janu'y, 1863
Private Henry M. Judy . . .	Surgeon's Cert. .	Janu'y, 1863
Private Stephen A Frailey . .	Ankle Dislocated	Febr'y, 1863
Private Robert Henderson . .	Wounds. . . .	March, 1863
Sergeant Henry Harris . . .	Surgeon's Cert. .	March, 1863
Serg't Carlisle L. Shackleford	Surgeon's Cert. .	March, 1863
Sergeant Henry H. Gabbard .	Surgeon's Cert. .	March, 1863
Private Ira G. Proffit	Surgeon's Cert. .	March, 1863
Private George W. Conner. .	Surgeon's Cert. .	April, 1863
Private Henry Burris	Surgeon's Cert. .	June, 1863
Private Milton Smith	Surgeon's Cert. .	June, 1863
Private Joseph McQueen. . .	Physical Disability	July, 1863
Sergeant DeWitt C. Winbourn	Wounds	August, 1863
Corporal Simpson Wood. . .	Surgeon's Cert. .	Janu'y, 1863
Sergeant Fielding P. Wood .	Consolidation . .	May, 1864
Musician Moses Whisman . .	Physical Disability	May, 1863

RE-ENLISTED AND LEFT AT CHATTANOOGA, TENNESSEE, NOVEMBER, 18TH, 1864.

NAMES.	AGE	COUNTY FROM
Sergeant George F. Edwards	23	Clay County.
Sergeant Washington Hollon	23	Clay County.
Corporal John W. Harrison	22	Estill County.
Corporal Ambrose W. Logsdon	24	Estill County.
Corporal William S. Hilton	21	Owsley County.
Corporal William R. Coyle	31	Estill County.
Corporal William C. Lutes	21	Owsley County.
Corporal John W. Wise	21	Estill County.
Corporal Robert G. Ramsey	21	Clay County.
Private James M. Whisman	24	Clay County.
Private Howard N. Burgess	20	Madison County.
Private Calaway Bowman	22	Owsley County.
Private Greenbury Bowman	21	Owsley County.
Private Elisha Bailey	27	Harlin County.
Private Garland Conner	20	Estill County.
Private Braxton D. Cox	21	Owsley County.
Private Alexander F. Hays	23	Knox County.
Private John D. Jamison	21	Owsley County.
Private George W. Jewell	21	Indiana.
Private Edward Lynch	22	Estill County.
Private Isaac T. Lamb	21	Madison County.
Private William C Lamb	22	Madison County.
Private James McLaughlin	38	Wakesford, Ind.
Private Harden Moore	24	Owsley County.
Private Randal M. Olinger	27	Lee County.
Private William L. Rice	33	Madison County.
Private John H. Stout	21	Clay County.
Private James Smith	22	Owsley County.
Private Eli A. Sparks	23	Estill County.
Private John Selby	20	Madison County.
Private Jonathan Scarbraugh	24	Madison County.
Private Elliott Turner	29	Breathitt County.
Private Wilbourn Turner	21	Breathitt County.
Private Christopher C. Webb	22	Estill County.
Private James F. Baker	23	Clay County.
Private Robert D. Harris	19	Estill County.
Private James Spencer	25	Perry County.

APPENDIX. 281

DIED.

NAMES.	CAUSE.	PLACE.	DATE.
Captain Landon C. Minter	Wounds	Murfreesboro	Jan. '63
Lieut. Wade B. Cox...	Wounds	Murfreesboro	Jan. '63
Lieut. Newton J. Hughes	Fever	Murfreesboro	Feb. '63
Sergt. Nathan C. Wilson	Fever	Lebanon, Ky.	Jan. '62
Sergt. Charles F. Culton	Fever	Lebanon	Jan. '62
Sergt. Hamilton W. Wright	Wounds	Murfreesboro	Jan. '63
Corp'l Alexander J. Baker	Fever	Lebanon	Jan. '62
Corporal John H. Powell	Fever	Lebanon	Jan. '62
Corp'l Franklin J. Hughes	Fever	Nashville	Sept. '62
Corp'l Isaac H. Anderson	Diarrhea	Nashville	Oct. '62
Corp'l Abner Q. Logsdon	Wound	Chattanooga	Oct. '63
Corporal James C. Tolson	Smallpox	Louisville	Dec. '63
Private Joseph King...	Fever	Lebanon	Jan. '62
Private Greenbury King	Fever	Lebanon	Jan. '62
Private Jonn D. Williams	Fever	Lebanon	Jan. '62
Private Wm. Hembree	Fever	Lebanon	Jan. '62
Private John Roberts	Fever	Lebanon	Jan. '62
Private Jesse Coomer...	Fever	Lebanon	Jan. '62
Private Elisha Mayo...	Hemorrh'ge	Lebanon	Feb. '62
Private William Smith..	Fever	Lebanon	Feb. '62
Musician Richard Poore	Inf. Lungs.	Lebanon	Mar. '62
Private Buford Lutes...	Jaundice	Lebanon	Mar. '62
Private Isaac Roberds	Fever	Lebanon	Mar. '62
Private Uriah King	Typh. Fever	Lebanon	Mar. '62
Private Ira G. Dixon...	Fever	Lebanon	Mar. '62
Private Charles N. Burgess	Diarrhea	Richmond,Ky	April '62
Private Butler Frailey	Wounds	Nashville	Dec. '62
Private Fletcher Bowman	Wound	Murfreesboro	Jan. '63
Private Isaac Thomas	Wound	Murfreesboro	Jan. '63
Private John R. Wilson	Wound	Murfreesboro	Feb. '63
Priv. Edward Richardson	Fever	Murfreesboro	Feb. '63
Private Andrew Vaughn	Dropsy	Murfreesboro	May '63
Private Alexander Gibson	Killed	Chickamauga	Sept. '63
Private John W. Barnett	Varioloid	Nashville	Nov. '63

NOTE.—The author regrets being unable to obtain copies of muster-out rolls of other companies in time for the publisher.

The general readers of history are familiar with Sherman's triumphant march to the sea, with Gen. Hood's defeat before Nashville, the early spring campaign of 1865, with the closing scenes of the war by the surrender of Lee's army at Appomattox, Va., in April, immediately followed by the surrender of Johnson's and Kirby Smith's armies. Thus closed a war which had extended over a period of four years, had caused more lavish expenditure of money, and mustered into the field a larger force than any war of modern times. Hundreds of thousands had been slain and died from exposure, sickness and bad treatment in southern prisons. Slavery, the boasted chief corner-stone of the defunct confederacy had been effectually annihilated, and the southern leaders and many of their followers humbled but somewhat sullen.

The people of the north, and many of the inhabitants of the border states, in the midst of their rejoicing, were shocked at the news of the assassination of President Lincoln by a tool of the expiring confederacy. Then occurred much loud talk in high places of "punishing traitors and making treason odious," but these vaporings cooled down. Jeff. Davis, the arch-traitor, was set free, and the great question that puzzled our president and congress was, what course the government should pursue in regard to the late rebellious states. Andrew Johnson, Lincoln's successor, "swung around the circle," and took opposite views to our national legislators; but no one was punished except a few of the assassin

Booth's co-conspirators and Wertz. The bungling reconstruction acts were followed with unsatisfactory results to both north and south.

The ratification of the fifteenth amendment to the United States constitution, giving the ballot to the colored men, was especially distasteful to the ex-rebels. Ninety-five out of every hundred of these newly made citizens could not read their ballots, the greater number being entirely dependent upon the white land-owners, who, seeing their only chance of regaining any political control in the government was to use this blind power, and, with the help of the Democratic party in the north, these ex-rebels yet hoped to gain by the ballot what they failed to do by the bullet, i. e., control of the government, and how near they came, through their Mississippi plans, and the help of hungry northern Democratic politicians, to making their threat good, are matters of very recent date.

But the recent presidential election has demonstrated conclusively that the Democratic party, though boasting of a "Solid South," can never gain a national victory again. The youth of this republic are not democratic, and so long as slavery and the war linger within the memory of our youth, the republic will continue to grow up republicans, and slavery and the war will be remembered as long as our public school system exists. A pointed editorial in a leading democratic paper of Chicago, just after this last national contest (1880), coincides so nearly with our views on this subject that we give it here, in hopes that my old soldier brothers' boys who may chance to read this little volume may reason and reflect on the truth or falsity of the cause of the Democrats' late defeat:

It is vain for statesmen to declare that there were as many Democrats as Republicans in the Union army. It is vain to affirm that the war for the preservation of the Union could not have been carried to a successful close without the assistance of the Democratic party. It is idle for philanthropy to suggest that the attitude of the party toward the war in the beginning was a humane one; that it was inspired by the higher and better wish that the cause of the conflict should be peaceably removed, and the spilling of brother's blood by brother's hands avoided. The Democratic party has been ideally identified with slavery and slave-holding. The Republican party is ideally identified with emancipation and the war; therefore is the youth of the country incapable of being Democratic— therefore the Democratic party can never win a national victory. Its old men are dying away; the boys who catch the ballots that fall from their stiffened hands are Republicans. The young wife who held the babe up to kiss the father as he hurried to the tap of his departing regiment has not suckled a Democrat. The weary foot of the gray grandmother, who watched the children while the wife was busy, has not rocked the cradle of a Democrat. The chair that the soldier-father never came back to fill has never been climbed upon by Democrats. The old blue coat that his comrades carried back was cut up for little jackets, but not one enclosed the heart of a Democrat. The rattled musket that fell from him with his last shot became the thoughtless toy of his boys, but not a hand that played with it was the hand of a Democrat. The babe he kissed crowed and crowed for his return, and its unwitting and unanswered notes were not from the throat of a Democrat. The tear-soiled camp letters which the mother read aloud in the long bitter evenings, while the boys clustered at her knees, did not fall upon Democratic ears. The girls' sobs, blended with the mother's weeping, did not make Democrats of their brothers. Perhaps the father had been a Democrat all his life. The children go to school; there is not a Democrat on its benches. The First Reader contains the portrait of Abraham Lincoln; that kind and sturdy face never made a Democrat. On its simple pages, in words of one or two syllables, is told the story of his birth and death; that story never made a Democrat. In the pranks of the play-ground the name silences the frolicsome, and makes the jolliest grave ; that name never made a Democrat. In the pictures that light up the geography are the firing on Fort Sumter and the death of Ellsworth ; those pictures make no Democrats. The first page of the history contains a representation of the surrender of Lee at Appomattox ; no boy sets eyes on that and after avows himself a Democrat. In the higher grade the same subtle and irresistible influence is at work. The text books contain extracts from patriot speeches during the war; those speeches make no Democrats. The great battles are briefly described; the narrative has no Democratic listeners. The strain of martial music runs through the readers, and that music makes no Democrats. Sketches of the great generals are given ; their deeds arouse the enthusiasm of the lads, but there is no Democrat among them. The horrors and sufferings of the slaves are told ; the maddened blood that mounts the boy's cheek is not Democratic blood. The curse of slavery has pursued the Democratic party, and has hounded it to its death ; therefore let it die, and no lip will be found to say a prayer over the grass of its grave. The late defeat need not be attributed to any other cause. Other causes have been at work, but they were only incidental. The tariff was one; sectionalism was a second; let well-enough alone was a third; the October elections in Indiana was a fourth. But all these are trivial, and together could not have accomplished the result. The result was accomplished because the youth of the republic are not Democratic. That party is therefore without a future and without a hope. The maledictions of the war have falsified its brain; the curse of slavery has poisoned its blood and rotted its bone. Let it die.

In looking back twenty years, and noting the unparalleled development of our great Northwest, and the general prosperity of our common country, the rapid extinguishment of the national debt, the credit and respect other nations of the world have for Americans, and our free institutions, we cannot help but feel proud of our glorious Union of States, and in conclusion, say to all that may have been in arms against the boys in blue, during the bloody days of which this volume treats, or to those whose sympathies were more with the gray than for us, mourn not over the death of slavery, which has been the curse of our country, cease your vain regrets for the "lost cause," stop your efforts to keep alive the once dangerous but now defunct principles for which Lee and Jackson fought, and learn again to love and respect the one flag of liberty and the one great country it represents. Unite your energies in helping to develop the vast hidden resources of wealth of the sunny South; declare that labor shall be respected, instead of despised; discard old time prejudices, abolish class distinction among whites, encourage public schools, where all, however poor or of what race or color, may have free access to the tree of knowledge, that intelligence may wield the ballot. Then strive for a "free ballot and a fair count," and with us old boys of the blue rejoice in and be proud of a government where the humblest laborer can go to his cabin after his day's labor, and take his little towheaded boy on his knee and tell him he has the future and the public schools before him, and has just as good chances to be President of the United States as any other boy. Let us throw away section lines and sectionalism, now the curse of slavery is out of the way, and turn our attention to watching our common interests, and guarding against other evils that may be threatening our liberties and our peace, such as the encroachments of powerful monopolies and the fearful increase of vice and intemperance, that we may be able at no distant day to say that all our labors have not been in vain.

www.ingramcontent.com/pod-product-compliance
Lightning Source LLC
Chambersburg PA
CBHW031338230426
43670CB00006B/365